ASPATORE BOOKS

About Aspatore Books
www.Aspatore.com

Aspatore Books has become one of the leading book publishing houses in record setting time by combining the best aspects of traditional book publishing with the new abilities enabled by the Internet and technology. Aspatore Books publishes the Inside the Minds, Bigwig Briefs, OneHourWiz and Aspatore Business Review imprints in addition to other best selling non-fiction and fiction books. Aspatore Books is focused on infusing creativity, innovation and interaction into the book publishing industry and providing a heightened experience for readers worldwide. Aspatore Books focuses on publishing traditional print books, while our two portfolio companies, Big Brand Books and Publishville.com focus on developing areas within the book publishing world. Aspatore Books is committed to providing our readers, authors, bookstores, distributors and customers with the highest quality books, book related services, and publishing execution available anywhere in the world.

About Big Brand Books

Big Brand Books assists leading companies and select individuals with book writing, publisher negotiations, book publishing, book sponsorship, worldwide book promotion and generating a new revenue stream from publishing. The goal of Big Brand Books is to help our clients capture the attention of prospective customers, retain loyal clients and penetrate new target markets by sharing valuable information in books and providing the highest quality content for readers worldwide. For more information please visit www.BigBrandBooks.com or email jonp@bigbrandbooks.com.

About Publishville.com

At Publishville.com, individuals worldwide can electronically publish books, articles, speeches, plays, reports, and more, set their own price, earn 50% royalties, and make a name for themselves. Publishville.com also features "The World's Most Intriguing Bookstore" which contains thousands of works from writers worldwide on every topic imaginable available only at Publishville.com.

INSIDE THE MINDS

Inside the Minds:
The Wireless Industry
*Industry Leaders Share Their Knowledge on the
Future of The Wireless Revolution*

**ASPATORE
BOOKS**

Published by Aspatore Books, Inc.
For information on bulk orders, sponsorship opportunities or any other questions please email sales@aspatore.com. For corrections, company/title updates, comments or any other inquiries please email info@aspatore.com.

First Printing, September 2001
10 9 8 7 6 5 4 3 2 1

Copyright © 2001 by Aspatore Books, Inc. All rights reserved. Printed in the United States of America. No part of this publication may be reproduced or distributed in any form or by any means, or stored in a database or retrieval system, except as permitted under Sections 107 or 108 of the United States Copyright Act, without prior written permission of the publisher.

ISBN 1-58762-020-0

Library of Congress Card Number: 2001090309

Cover design by Michael Lepera/Ariosto Graphics & James Weinberg

Material in this book is for educational purposes only. This book is sold with the understanding that neither any of the interviewees or the publisher is engaged in rendering legal, accounting, investment, or any other professional service.

This book is printed on acid free paper.

A special thanks to all the individuals that made this book possible.

Special thanks also to: Brigeth Rivera, Kirsten Catanzano, Susan Chernauskas, Melissa Conradi and especially Ted Juliano (Managing Editor)

The views expressed by the individuals in this book do not necessarily reflect the views shared by the companies they are employed by (or the companies mentioned in this book). The companies referenced may not be the same company that the individual works for since the publishing of this book.

About Inside the Minds

Become a Part of *Inside the Minds*

Ask a Question in an Upcoming Book, Nominate an Executive, Post Comments on the Topics Mentioned, Read Expanded Excerpts, Free Excerpts From Upcoming Books

www.InsideTheMinds.com

Inside the Minds was conceived in order to give readers actual insights into the leading minds of business executives worldwide. Because so few books or other publications are actually written by executives in industry, *Inside the Minds* presents an unprecedented look at various industries and professions never before available. In addition, the *Inside the Minds* web site makes the reading experience interactive by enabling readers to post messages and interact with each other, ask questions in upcoming books, read expanded comments on the topics covered and nominate individuals for upcoming books. *Inside the Minds* is now expanding the series to share the wealth of knowledge locked inside the minds of leading executives in every industry worldwide.

Also from Aspatore Books:
Bigwig Briefs
Condensed Business Intelligence From Industry Insiders

Become a Part of *Bigwig Briefs*

Publish a Knowledge Excerpt on an Upcoming Topic (50-5,000 words), Submit an Idea to Write an Entire Bigwig Brief, Post Comments on the Topics Mentioned, Read Expanded Excerpts, Free Excerpts From Upcoming Briefs

www.BigwigBriefs.com

Bigwig Briefs features condensed business intelligence from industry insiders and are the best way for business professionals to stay on top of the most pressing issues. There are two types of *Bigwig Briefs* books: the first is a compilation of excerpts from various executives on a topic, while the other is a book written solely by one individual on a specific topic. *Bigwig Briefs* is also the first interactive book series for business professionals whereby individuals can submit excerpts (50 to 5,000 words) for upcoming briefs on a topic they are knowledgeable on (submissions must be accepted by our editorial review committee and if accepted they receive a free copy of the book) or submit an idea to write an entire Bigwig Brief (accepted ideas/manuscripts receive a standard royalty deal). *Bigwig Briefs* is revolutionizing the business book market by providing the highest quality content in the most condensed format possible for business book readers worldwide.

ASPATORE
BUSINESS REVIEW

The Quarterly Book Featuring Excerpts From the Best Business Books

Aspatore Business Review is the perfect way for busy professionals to stay on top of the most pressing business issues. Each *Aspatore Business Review* includes knowledge excerpts and highlights from best selling business books, in-depth interviews with leading executives, and special features on emerging issues in the workplace. Every quarter, *Aspatore Business Review* brings you the most important excerpts from the best business books on topics such as:

- Management and Leadership
- Technology and the Internet
- Team Building
- Financial Accountability
- Staying ahead of Changing Markets
- Fostering Innovation
- Brand Building

Aspatore Business Review is the one book every business professional should read, and is the best way to keep current with your business reading in the most time efficient manner possible.

Subscribe today to Aspatore Business Review

www.Aspatore.com

ORDER THESE OTHER GREAT BOOKS TODAY!
Great for Yourself or Your Entire Team
Visit Your Local Bookseller Today!

Inside the Minds: Internet Bigwigs
Industry Experts Forecast the Future of the Internet Economy - *Inside the Minds: Internet Bigwigs* includes interviews with a handful of the leading minds of the Internet and technology revolution. These individuals include executives from Excite (Founder), Beenz.com (CEO), Organic (CEO), Agency.com (Founder), Egghead (CEO), Credite Suisse First Boston (Internet Analyst), CIBC (Internet Analyst) and Sandbox.com. Items discussed include killer-apps for the 21st century, the stock market, emerging industries, international opportunities, and a plethora of other issues affecting anyone with a "vested interest" in the Internet and technology revolution. $27.95

Inside the Minds: Leading Women
What it Takes for Women to Succeed and Have it All in the 21st Century - *Inside the Minds: Leading Women* includes interviews with CEOs and executives from companies such as Prudential, Women's Financial Network, SiliconSalley.com, Barclays Global Investors, RealEco.com, AgentArts, Kovair, MsMoney.com, LevelEdge and AudioBasket. These highly acclaimed women explain how to balance personal and professional lives, set goals, network, start a new company, learn the right skills for career advancement and more. $27.95

Inside the Minds: Internet Marketing
Industry Experts Reveal the Secrets to Marketing, Advertising, and Building a Successful Brand on the Internet - *Inside the Minds: Internet Marketing* includes interviews with leading marketing VPs from some of the top Internet companies in the world including Buy.com, 24/7 Media, DoubleClick, Guerrilla Marketing, Viant, MicroStrategy, MyPoints.com, WineShopper.com, Advertising.com and eWanted.com. Their experiences, advice, and stories provide an unprecedented look at the various online and offline strategies involved with building a successful brand on the Internet for companies in every industry. Also examined is calculating return on investment, taking an offline brand online, taking an online brand offline, where the future of Internet marketing is heading, and numerous other issues. $27.95

Inside the Minds: Venture Capitalists
Inside the High Stakes and Fast Paced World of Venture Capital - *Inside the Minds: Venture Capitalists* includes interviews with leading partners from Softbank, ICG, Sequoia Capital, CMGI, New Enterprise Associates, Bertelsmann Ventures, TA Associates, Kestrel Venture Management, Blue Rock Capital, Novak Biddle Venture Partners, Mid-Atlantic Venture Funds, Safeguard Scientific, Divine interVentures, and Boston Capital Ventures. Learn how some of the best minds behind the Internet revolution value companies, assess business models, and identify opportunities in the marketplace. $27.95

Inside the Minds: The Wireless Industry
Industry Leaders Discuss the Future of the Wireless Revolution - *Inside the Minds: The Wireless Industry* includes interviews with leading CEOs from companies such as AT & T Wireless, Omnisky, Wildblue, AirPrime, Digital Wireless, Aperto Networks, Air2Web, LGC Wireless, Arraycomm, Informio and Extenta. Items discussed include the future of the wireless industry, wireless devices, killer-apps in the wireless industry, the international landscape, government issues and more. $27.95

Inside the Minds: The New Health Care Industry
Industry Leaders Discuss the Internet Health Care Revolution - *Inside the Minds: The New Health Care Industry* includes interviews with leading CEOs from companies such as iMcKesson, Medscape, Adam.com, PhaseForward, AthenaHealth.com, HealthGrades, Oncology.com, Scheduling.com, eHealthInsurance and HealthGate Data. Items discussed include the effect of technology on the health care industry, future killer-apps, privacy issues, and the future of health care for patients. $27.95

Inside the Minds: Internet CFOs
Information Every Entrepreneur, Employee, Investor, and Services Professional Should Know About the Financial Side of Internet Companies – *Inside the Minds: Internet CFOs* includes interviews with leading CFOs from Hoovers, CBS Marketwatch, Register.com, eMusic.com webMethods, Ashford.com, Agillion.com, LivePerson, Nerve.com and Edgar Online. Items discussed include the way Internet companies are valued today and in the future, stock options, and financial trends affecting Internet companies at every level. $27.95

Inside the Minds: Internet BizDev
Industry Experts Reveal the Secrets to Inking Deals in the Internet Industry - *Inside the Minds: Internet BizDev* includes interviews with leading business development executives from companies such as Imandi, Real Names, yesmail.com, Netcreations, LifeMinders, Digital Owl, WebCT and Keen.com. Items discussed include calculating potential return on investment, partnership strategies, joint ventures, and where the future of Internet business development is heading among numerous other issues. $27.95

Inside the Minds: Chief Technology Officers
Industry Experts Reveal the Secrets to Developing, Implementing, and Capitalizing on the Best Technologies in the World - *Inside the Minds: Chief Technology Officers* includes interviews with leading technology executives from companies such as Engage, Datek, Symantec, Verisign, Vignette, WebMD, SONICblue, Kana Communications, Flooz.com and The Motley Fool. Their experiences, advice, and research provide an unprecedented look at the various strategies involved with developing, implementing, and capitalizing on the best technologies in the world for companies of every size and in every industry. $27.95

Inside the Minds: Internet Lawyers
The Most Up to Date Handbook of Important Answers to Issues Facing Every Entrepreneur, Lawyer, and Anyone with a Web Site – *Inside the Minds: Internet Lawyers* includes interviews with leading lawyers from some of the top Internet and technology focused law firms in the world. Items discussed include structuring ownership, raising money, venture capital, patents, intellectual property, forming the board, product liability, human resources, stock options, partnership contracts, privacy, and other issues that every business (and their lawyers) should be aware of. $27.95

Bigwig Briefs: Management & Leadership
Industry Experts Reveal the Secrets How to Get There, Stay There, and Empower Others That Work For You
Bigwig Briefs: Management & Leadership includes excerpts of advice from some of the leading executives in the business world. These highly acclaimed executives explain how to break into higher ranks of management, how to become invaluable to your company, and how to empower your team to perform to their utmost potential. (102 Pages) $14.95

Bigwig Briefs: Human Resources & Building a Winning Team
Industry Experts Reveal the Secrets to Hiring, Retaining Employees, Fostering Teamwork, and Building Winning Teams of All Sizes
Bigwig Briefs: Human Resources & Building a Winning Team includes excerpts of advice from some of the leading executives in the business world. These highly acclaimed executives explain the secrets behind hiring the best employees, incentivizing and retaining key employees, building teamwork, maintaining stability, encouraging innovation, and succeeding as a group. (102 Pages) $14.95

Bigwig Briefs: Online Advertising
Industry Experts Reveal the Secrets to Successful Online Advertising Programs
Bigwig Briefs: Online Advertising includes excerpts of advice from some of the leading marketing and advertising executives in the world. These highly acclaimed executives explain the secrets behind strategic planning, implementing, and maximizing your online advertising dollars. (102 Pages) $14.95

Bigwig Briefs: Startups Keys to Success
Industry Experts Reveal the Secrets to Launching a Successful New Venture
Bigwig Briefs: Startups Keys to Success includes excerpts of advice from some of the leading VCs, CEOs CFOs, CTOs and business executives in every industry. These highly acclaimed executives explain the secrets behind the financial, marketing, business development, legal, and technical aspects of starting a new venture. (102 Pages) $14.95

Bigwig Briefs: Small Business Internet Advisor
Industry Experts Reveal the Secrets to Internet Marketing, BizDev, HR, Financing, eCommerce and Other Important Topics Facing Every Small Business Doing Business on the Internet
Bigwig Briefs: Small Business Internet Advisor includes excerpts of advice from some of the leading executives in the world in every field of specialty. These highly acclaimed executives explain the secrets behind making the most of your small business online in a very easy to understand and straight forward fashion. (102 Pages) $14.95

Bigwig Briefs: The Golden Rules of the Internet Economy
Industry Experts Reveal the Best Advice Ever on Succeeding in the Internet Economy
Bigwig Briefs: The Golden Rules of the Internet Economy includes excerpts of advice from some of the leading business executives in the Internet and Technology industries. These highly acclaimed executives explain where the future of the Internet economy is heading, mistakes to avoid for companies of all sizes, and the keys to long term success. (102 Pages) $14.95

Go to www.InsidetheMinds.com for a Complete List of Titles!

Inside the Minds:
The Wireless Industry
Industry Leaders Share Their Knowledge on the Future of The Wireless Revolution

CONTENTS

John Zeglis, AT&T Wireless
Make It Simple — 17

Patrick McVeigh, OmniSky
Bringing Value to the Consumer — 33

Sanjoy Malik, Air2Web
Wireless Challenges — 49

Paul Sethy, AirPrime
The High Costs of Wireless — 61

Reza Ahy, Aperto Networks
Developing Areas of Wireless — 77

Martin Cooper, Arraycomm
The Real Potential for Wireless — 87

Robert Gemmell, Digital Wireless
Bringing Wireless Into the Mainstream — 107

Alex Laats, Informio
VoiceXML — 123

Rod Hoo, LGC Wireless
Reaching the Epitome of Productivity — 141

Scott Bradner, Harvard University
Identifying Revenue Opportunities — 153

Tom Moore, WildBlue
The Wireless Satellite Space — 173

JOHN ZEGLIS
Make It Simple
AT&T Wireless
CEO

Background Information

I have spent my entire professional adult life in and around telecommunications. I represented AT&T and the Bell System as counsel for 10 years. When the Bell system breakup occurred, I jumped over into AT&T, became its general counsel and then added responsibilities for government affairs, regulatory matters, public relations and strategy development. By the second half of the '90s I was in general management, and when Mike Armstrong arrived I became the President of AT&T. Then, about a year ago, I was designated the Chairman and CEO of our wireless tracker, soon to become AT&T Wireless, Inc.

On Change in the Industry

The part that's constant is change. If you go back over those years I just described, you'll see that my only constant is managing and, in more recent days, leading change. Telecom was a completely closed monopoly when I started. We had just received the very first regulatory decisions to make parts of the industry competitive.

What's constant is that the market opens and the technology moves on, and we've got to adapt everything from public policy to company strategy and structure in light of it. The most exciting thing now is that I'm part of a wireless industry that is fundamentally going to change the way people live through their communications. Wireless communications will eventually give each person access to all the people and all the information in the world.

Despite all the market change I mentioned, fundamental change in any industry – including telecom – is relatively rare. For the longest time you talked into the mouthpiece and it came out in the earpiece. You could price it differently and make the dialing automatic – but the essence was the same, you talked into the mouthpiece and listened through the earpiece.

You can have all of the functions of wired telephony and not have to stand 6 feet from the wall to get it at the end of a cord. You can take communications anywhere, anytime, anyplace on the earth; that is change. The other great change is you get more than talk. You get access to all the information in the world and the ability to manipulate it. Sometimes we call that the Internet. When you put those two fundamental changes together, you've got fusion. And with fusion you're going to create whole new elements. Now that is exciting.

On Growth of the Industry

I think it's what we refer to as wireless data or the mobile Internet. But the growth of the wireless Internet depends on how easy we can make it to use. Right now, all the human interface is on a pad, whether it's a touch pad or a

26-key pad. We're going to see a much easier human interaction – voice interfaces, speech synthesis and recognition – so information can come to you effortlessly. You'll request it with your voice and hear it through speech synthesis or somebody else's voice. Easy, intuitive, human-like access to all that information will be very important.

We're also going to see the mobile Internet deliver in ways that the wired Internet is quite challenged to match. You can deliver instant communications, instant information wherever you need it, wherever you are – it could be at a meeting, it could be in center field if you're in a summer softball league – but that's something that only the wireless Internet can do. You can't do that with a wired Internet.

Next, you're going to be able to tailor the information to exactly where you are. For example, you'll tell your phone, "I have no idea where I am, but I've got to go to the airport," and your wireless provider will know where you are because it's triangulating your position from their towers. We'll be able to give you the directions, show you pictures of where to turn, tell you what the road conditions are, estimate how long the drive is going to be, check your airplane and see if it's on time. We can gather all that information and tell you, "Relax, the plane is delayed, you don't have to leave for 45 minutes and when you do, take this route."

That kind of location-context instantly-tailored information is huge. But for it to work we have to make the experience extremely customer friendly in both the application and the interface. I suppose I can do everything I just described right now consulting a lot of different sites and doing a lot of inputs on my PocketNet or on anybody else's web, but what I want to be able to do is to tell the phone, "Newark Airport, Continental 547 tonight," and have it do the rest of the work for me.

Better yet, I want to see the day when my personal communications device will know when I'm flying out of Newark because I put the information in my electronic organizer and have it automatically call me with flight and traffic information at the right time and on the right day.

The Importance of Easy Interfaces

The most computer literate population will adapt and find ways to access the sizzle and all the great new applications, even among varied interfaces and protocols for accessing them. But to really drive wireless data applications and mobile Internet advantages deep into the population, an easy to use human interface is going to be extraordinarily important. So, yes, without ease-of-use we will limit our accessibility to just a small segment of the population. That's where we'd be with computers today if we hadn't evolved beyond punch cards and UNIX. But I think that within the decade we'll see an easy-to-use wireless interface that will connect us with people and information.

The Effect of Startups on the Market

When it comes to the wireless space, we're seeing both a bigger pie and more kinds of pies. I think it's a very healthy thing to have a lot of companies out there trying to develop different kinds of applications. I've lived through a lot of the not-invented-here syndrome during my time in the Bell System, and back then there wasn't any choice for voice or even for the color of your phone. So I'm a big fan of a frothy industry with a whole lot of players out there trying to come up with different applications. I want them to come around the operators, come around AT&T Wireless especially, and show their wares. I'm not going to keep our customers from reaching them. I'm not going to say, "You must only work within the walled garden of mobile Internet sites that I give you." We'll give our customers a great portal, we'll give them great customization, we hope they stay there for some of their use, but if they want to go to any other ASPs, any other mobile wireless site, we'll make that possible. It's good; it's healthy. There are too many possibilities for any one, two or three of us to think we can provide it all. I think we are going to see a lot of application development on the outside of the operators, and it's good for all of us.

Advice for Wireless Startups

I'd say make it so easy to use that a 3 year old could do it. Make your human interface the easiest in the industry. I can't evaluate whether your application for electronic coupons zapped to shoppers on Fifth Avenue in New York City is better than some other guy's application for folks caught on the turnpike trying to get to the airport. I don't know which is going to be more popular. I hope you all have popular applications. I think the winners are going to be the operators who say, "I have an easy customer interface, I have an easy to use application, so intuitive it takes no time to learn and of course delivers great value in the content itself." Make it easy, make it simple. We've got to stop entertaining ourselves with technology and wizardry. We've got to see how simple we can make it at the interface level. We can bury the gee whiz technology deep down, so I would tell any apps maker "Make it simple." If you can access it with six pushes, make it two, you get it down to two, make it one, you got it down to one, show me how I could do a voice interface with it.

The Availability of Capital

When it comes to the capital for the developers and the wireless ASPs, you're talking about an order of magnitude less than the capital required to do the applications I've just described. We operators can supply the location information, and with the software tools available and with the access to wired Internet technology, I don't think we'll see a problem with the capital to develop the cool applications.

A Path to Profitability

Each of those metrics is important in sequence and at the right time. In any startup business or startup market you want and expect to see the customers first and then you expect to see revenue. After a reasonable period, you expect to see cash flow generated, and at some point after the rapid growth phase you actually expect to see free cash flow and net income.

The industry is in the stages right now where the new PCS markets are beginning to break positive and those started two and a half, maybe three years ago. For the slightly more mature 850 cellular markets there is good EBITDA generation throughout the industry. So it just depends on where you are on the growth curve, where you are in the particular markets, whether you've just shown up, how much opportunity there is to penetrate more deeply, whether in subscribership or minutes. Happily, almost throughout our industry, we're still on the steep part of that technology adoption curve, so revenue and EBITDA generation are value drivers today.

Europe's Effect on the U.S. Wireless Industry

At this point I'm going to say that it gives us a comparative advantage against the rest of the world. Penetration rates have been slower to develop here. There are a whole lot of reasons for that: different standards, a confusing lack of interoperability in the early years of our industry, and the absence of a pre-paid product. You can see in many countries that as soon as you hit 25% demand explodes – the U.S. reached a 25% penetration rate in 1999.

In the U.S. we also have the advantage of people who use the phone a lot more than elsewhere. We have more minutes of use, and I think that's a tremendous advantage for the industry. People are used to communicating via wireless, and that's going to make an easier migration path for them to the wireless Internet. And these are the customers who are going to be most likely to migrate to the higher-value applications of wireless data.

Expanding the Use of Wireless

For interacting with people, namely for voice, it's going to take great coverage and quality. I do believe that people are going to move virtually all of their voice communication to wireless devices. But the substitution won't happen unless we give them outstanding coverage and quality.

We are going to move folks to predominantly wireless data usage. To do that it will take an outrageously easy-to-use, simple interface that gets exactly what you need tailored to your situation, your geography right now, bang, bang, bang. You don't use these devices to surf for 20 minutes and then assemble your own set of bookmarks or "ahahs" or discoveries. I'm on the move, I want to know what I need to know right now, the information is tailored to me and it's as easy to access as pressing that thumb button three times. It's as easy to program as an elevator. That's what it's going to take.

The industry has have done a great job with that in the voice world. Any 3-year-old at home can activate a worldwide-automated long-distance dialing system, 15 punches of the keypad and you're into Slovenia. Three punches and you're into emergency services. It's harder to do in data, probably even harder in wireless data, but it's that ultimate simplicity coupled with tailoring the information to personal needs and giving it to you wherever you travel. That's what it's going to take to make wireless data overwhelm the wired Internet, but I believe we'll do it.

Issues Facing the Wireless Industry

We've got an overwhelming demand, or an overwhelming need, to keep up with capacity. We're on the steep part of the technology curve, with more than 20 million new units coming into the industry every year. Just to put this in perspective, it is as if every man, woman, and child in Australia moves to the U.S. every year and is given a mobile phone and starts calling. That's how large the capacity challenge is to the industry.

In the wired world, it was 85 years from the invention of the telephone before we installed a whole 1 million lines in a single year. The top year was in 1996, with 16 million new lines, and estimates for the wireless industry are that it will add more than 20 million new channels annually, for the next few years, and we'll see what happens after that. So the big challenge is keeping up with that demand so that the customer doesn't get dropped or blocked. .

The related challenge, and this applies to wireless data as well, is enough spectrum. This country works with less commercially-available spectrum than other countries that have been leading the wireless revolution.

Our government has got to catch up to the rest of the world and make additional spectrum available. The truth is that Western Europe and Asia both make more available to their operators than we do in this country. And I'm not critical of either the FCC Chairman or the President. They've both been out recently saying they recognize this, and they're going to work on it, that it's a tough problem.

The Optimal Wireless Environment

What I would like to happen is to get that extra spectrum out into the market, I'd relocate some of the broadcasters, and I'd relocate a lot of the military out of the most popular bands that are available in the rest of the world. Beyond that, being in the mainstream of world technology development really counts here. It means that you can ride on everybody else's R & D. That's why the overwhelming majority in the world uses GSM. Until recently, carriers in the U.S. have largely used TDMA or CDMA.

Further, I think the importance of the mainstream includes where in the spectrum your country locates your commercial mobile operators. So it's not just any spectrum, it's spectrum that approaches what's used in the rest of the world. I think that's very important. And once the spectrum is out there I'd make it freely leaseable and salable. I wouldn't clog the wheels of spectrum commerce, so to speak, with a whole lot of government regulation and restriction. Get it out there and let the market take care of getting it into the hands of the people who can most effectively use it.

Expectations for Wireless

Let's not forget voice. People like to talk to one another, so as important as I think it is to take this to a new level in the mobile Internet, we're not going to neglect great voice quality service. That's application number one. I resist trying to predict the killer app for the mobile Internet because my concept is a little different. We're going to give you access to all the people in the world and all the information in the world wherever you are, and we're going to let it appear on any mobile device you have or any mobile device you want to carry around your house. Those are your Legos, and you put them together in any way you find useful. That's your killer app.

That said, you can understand a hierarchy of wireless applications developing on our mobile devices. The first one is pretty clearly communications – instant information transmitted to me whenever I need it, transmitted back to anybody who needs a response.

Messaging brings instantly useful information – pushing a stock quote at me, pushing a meeting date and time at me, having me respond from the two-way SMS phones or from my web phone. That kind of instantly useful information and response would seem to be the earliest app.

Then you've got to kick it up to a level where information is delivered to you in the context of where you stand, and it creates useful information because of where you are. If you're in a department store and you're thinking about buying a flat screen TV, instantly useful information from my mobile device means that I can swipe the barcode and immediately get this information. I can see consumer reports on that particular flat screen TV. I can also press "*" and I can find where else within 10 miles of where I stand that same flat panel display is sold, I can see what the prices are, I can ask for phone numbers and directions to those other places, I can see what kind of coupons have electronically flashed on my screen just because I'm walking around the mall and happen to be near Macy's, and I can make my purchase choice right there. That's because the information was immediately adapted to where I was. I was looking at an appliance, got information on that appliance, got comparative information and directions everywhere else for 10 miles, and I chose to buy that one and zapped it with my phone. The phone became my electronic wallet and I walked away.

Then we're going to get into the stream of commerce. We're going to put those coupons on your phone as you walk by department stores. The coupons will only be good for 90 minutes; so come on in and shop. And merchants will know who is walking by their stores and they'll be able to send coupons targeted to me. When I walk by Circuit City, they'll know I buy a lot of CDs and send me coupons for the latest classical releases. Of course if you're someone who doesn't want merchants to know where you're walking, that's fine. We'll always give you the choice to opt out.

Then there are those refrigerators that are supposed to read bar codes that show me on the outside of the refrigerator door whether I'm low on milk. I consider those primitive. I want that information flashing on my car dashboard when I'm driving home from work and about to pass a grocery store. I want to be reminded that I'm low on milk when I can do something about it. And I want to be able to press one more button so the grocery store has milk waiting for me as I pull up to the drive-through.

And then you're going to kick it on to another level where all of that interaction is done within the network and information is pretty much delivered below the surface of my conscious by the machines in the network.

The Integration of Voice and Wireless

Voice is going to be an important application for a long time. The untethered, always reachable aspect of wireless is going to make it that much more valuable, but that's not cutting edge. What we're going to create is the ability to have information anywhere, what I've been referring to as the mobile Internet. Now that I can have information anywhere, how do I get it? I can do it on a telephone screen, I can do it on a palm screen, I can do it on a screen for appliances yet to be invented and there are a lot of those.

I'm not suggesting that the voice application is the future. I'm saying that we can take this to new and better places when we marry data with mobility. I'm saying that some people will want to access that new advantage on the key pad, but others who may not be as comfortable will find advantage in accessing it through their own voice and hearing it back through another voice, and this is what makes markets. We want to be ready and able to serve them all. For us to take the whole of the country off of the wires, we're really going to have to provide multiple interfaces for people who prefer to do it different ways.

On Leadership

Ultimately, all leaders have something to contribute substantively, but I think fundamentally before you make your own substantive contribution, you have to chart a direction, get people excited and aligned with it, and make it a lot of fun for everybody to go charging out there and achieve the vision.

Alignment around a shared objective is absolutely critical. Making work fun is essential to release high energy. And leaders must also bring substantive contributions of their own, whether it's analyses or sales or insight or technological innovation. Leaders can't just be "enablers" or mere "managers."

It all starts with somebody saying, "I see a destination, I see a vision, I see objectives." Then working with their team, getting input, adapting and adjusting and saying, "All right, there it is, let's get all the noses pointed in the same direction and go for it." If you can do that and make it fun for them, there's no stopping that kind of team.

Three Key Steps for Wireless

First, we want to take wireless to a new place, beyond voice and into the mobile Internet, and give that same untethered advantage to folks for reaching data and information as they have now for their voice communications. Second we'll do that with ubiquitous coverage, high quality services, and great customer care for folks who need a little help. Finally, we'll do it with the globe's easiest customer interface, just as we did for voice dialing.

Then we can really change the world. And then with access to all the world's people and all the world's information, the world can change us. And that's a cycle of change that's something to really get excited about.

A native of Momence, Illinois, Zeglis spent his undergraduate years at the University of Illinois, and is a 1972 magna cum laude graduate of Harvard Law School. He was a senior editor of the Harvard Law Review and won a Knox Memorial Fellowship for a year of postgraduate study in law and economics in Europe.

Zeglis, 52, began his career in law in 1973 as an associate with Sidley & Austin. He became partner in 1978, and on January 1, 1984, he joined AT&T as corporate vice president - law. Zeglis was named AT&T's general counsel in 1986. While retaining that title he served in a series of executive assignments with increasing responsibility before being elected vice chairman in June 1997. Later that year, he was named president.

While president, Zeglis was responsible for AT&T's wireless, consumer and international businesses. During his tenure, the company launched several successful campaigns, including AT&T Digital One Rate, the first national flat-rate wireless calling plan, and the AT&T One Rate 7 Cent consumer long distance offer. He was also responsible for developing the AT&T and BT relationship that led to the formation of Concert, a global venture of the two companies.

Zeglis is a member of the American Bar Association and state and local bar associations and professional groups, and is active in volunteer groups supporting education.

The Wireless Industry

He is chairman of the board of trustees of George Washington University, a trustee of the Culver Education Foundation, Culver, Indiana, and a trustee of the United Negro College Fund, New York. Zeglis is a member of the University of Illinois Business Advisory Council and serves on the board of the Rural School and Community Trust, Washington, D.C.

He is a director of the Helmerich and Payne Corporation in Tulsa and the Sara Lee Corporation, Chicago.

PATRICK MCVEIGH
Bringing Value to the Consumer
OmniSky
Chairman and CEO

The Evolution of Wireless

Let's step back and talk about what we're trying to accomplish here. On the one hand, wireless data is not new, it's been around a long time: your FedEx driver, your UPS driver, your guy that's wearing that ray gun in a warehouse scanning everything, they're all using wireless. Those vertical applications have been out there. What's new is enabling a broader set of applications that people can use. Traditionally, whether you look at Palm or cell phones in the beginning, who are the first people that tend to adopt these things? First there are the geeks and then the early adopters, and who do the early adopters tend to be? They tend to be business people, right? Business people looking for an edge, looking for a tool that helps them. Certainly I think that there are very clear killer apps that are well demonstrated, mail and messaging for example. Kids in the U.S. have been using pagers for years, and now it's interactive. Now it has some content, and we know how addicted teenagers can get to messaging, we've seen that with AOL. I think that's a step, but what we're really talking about here isn't just that; it's really leveraging the Internet itself. How do we extend that to the wireless mode in a way that is optimized for smaller mobile devices, mobile devices that have less capability because of bandwidth size and less processing power because batteries are a limiting factor? On the other hand, how do we make it feel enough like the Internet they're used to and provide more of that richness? That's been one of the challenges for the WAP experience: it's been too austere, too hard to use, not to mention connection time is too expensive. And because we have this new kind of platform there are all kinds of new services that don't make a lot of sense on a stationary PC or even a laptop – things that take into account location, things that take into account different types of notification – that do make sense when you're mobile.

Your handheld device is always on and always with you. We know we can start to give it a whole new kind of intelligence to help you through your day. That's the vision. How do we take Internet components that we know and love now, like mail and messaging, and add location, community, content and commerce into that mix? The key to the mobile platform right now is providing a great core experience and we've certainly focused on that.

A great experience with valuable services that people will use is the beginning, and developing those service requires an open platform. IP-based packet networks are key for the long term. It's not so much a matter of sitting down and figuring out what the next killer applications in content are, but rather having a model that encourages other people to create new applications for the service. That was the nature of the PC. The PC quickly progressed beyond the vision of its creator. I think the same holds true for the handheld. We're going to find the same thing on the mobile Internet, which means we've got to create a platform that's robust yet handles the trade-offs demanded by mobility that ultimately lets people create new applications and new services. We are going to get surprised here, we're going to see an application and once we see it we'll say, "Well of course, that makes perfect sense."

The Profitability of Wireless

In the handheld space a lot of the networks will converge voice and data services. We think there will be both converged devices and diverged devices, particularly when you start to look at Bluetooth, where you could have a wireless Bluetooth headset connected to a data tablet, or you could have a wireless Bluetooth phone. We do believe the interaction of voice and data services are important, but we think customers will have more choices. Remember the impact of the cellular phone form factor on the sales of that phone. If cellular phones were still bricks, I guarantee you we wouldn't have hundreds of millions of them in the marketplace. People would say, I'm not going to carry this, voice is important but I'm just not going to carry a brick.

Where do people make money? Clearly one of the most efficient areas is subscription fees. Right now in the U.S. when people think of data services they like to think of the basic service having a flat rate, sort of an all you can eat. Why? Well, for one thing it's what they're used to. For another thing, they get very nervous if the data service is drawing from their voice bucket because they don't exactly have the same understanding of Web time. If I'm on the phone five minutes, that's easy to understand, I use five of my 2000 minutes, but if I'm on the Web I'm not as aware of that. For this reason, we'll see that model vary from place to place around the world.

There are also certain value added services that people will pay for, such as enterprise email behind a fire wall. We think that commerce can be an important source of revenue, m-commerce, e-commerce, whatever you want to call it. Imagine yourself buying a book at Barnes & Noble on your computer, and your profile information isn't already stored with them. If you're trying to do it on a mobile device, the reality is you're probably not willing to endure as many steps as you will on your PC. The device is smaller, you're in a more mobile mode. The key for commerce to work is something we're working on: we've undertaken an initiative called One Tap, which integrates the functionality of the handheld and the opportunity of services to simplify transactions. I should be able to see something, tap once or twice and buy it. We believe that if we can simplify that process that's going to be an important source of revenue because we will have, and already have, merchants who share portions of transactions with us because we've made it so accessible to the customer.

Advertising is a little tougher. You don't have the real estate, and you don't want the person to throw the device in the garbage because the obnoxious factor is going through the roof. It has to be done in a way that's very helpful to the user. For instance, I'm standing on a street corner during the holidays in New York and I'm with three friends, and every restaurant is booked but I want to know if we can get a great Italian meal that's not too far away. If I could provide them with that information in a way that will be an enormous service to them, and lets me make money in the process, then that's interesting. I don't think, though, that users will put up with the notion of churning up coupons as you walk down the street. I think there's an opportunity there; in fact we've formed a consortium with Double Click to really go after the whole mobile advertising opportunity, but I think it's going to be a little bit different than what we've seen on the Web. It will not be loads of banners coming across; it has to be done in a more sensitive way. Mobile devices are like people crossing the desert, they throw things away that are weighty the further out they go.

People are making a real trade-off; they're saying I'm going to carry this thing so it better be valuable. Phones finally got to the point where they're small enough that people could compare them favorably to the pagers they'd been wearing for 10-15 years. Now instead of a pager I just carry my phone. It's small enough, it's wearable, coverage is good enough. So where do you make money? The subscription model is definitely a direction many will go in this space and we think that will continue in various forms. I think there are various services we can monetize, such as value added services and commerce through transactions, and I think there is an opportunity to monetize some advertising. We also believe one of the up and coming value added services is gaming.

It's very clear that messaging and community are already very, very important on mobile devices. Some of the things we've seen on i-Mode would indicate that, so it's not an enormous leap to imagine that gaming will be the next step on handheld devices in the U.S. These games are completely addictive. I think we're going to see some very cool things in that space, where people are going to end up with kind of the thumb version of tennis elbow again.

Obstacles to Wireless

One, we need to get our next generation networks built out. That, of course, is a bigger challenge in the U.S. in particular because of the geography and the fact that we have a number of standards.

The second factor is the devices. Again I go back to the cell phone. The first cell phones were storage batteries with a handset connected by a wire, then eventually you got those first Motorola handhelds that were brick size, and now people look at the old phones and think they're really clunky. Now we have the new Ericsson or the new Nokia phones; they've become these wearable things and that has made an enormous difference. The same thing needs to happen with mobile email and Internet devices. Obviously we need to maintain a certain amount of screen real estate, but in terms of ruggedness, in terms of thinness, it has to improve significantly. If I could give you something that had the screen real estate of a Palm yet was incredibly thin and flexible and rugged so that you could throw it in your pocket and if you sat on it you wouldn't kill it, that would make an enormous difference. Think about what happened when we had great TFT screens on laptops, it changed the business. Suddenly people said I can do real work on this, so screen technology and form factor on devices are really important.

I think the third thing is we need to continue to drive toward ever-improved services. We need to give people access to the information that's most important to them, whether it's mail, or AOL Instant Messenger, any of those core things that are now getting used for communicating. We need to extend those into the mobile world in smart ways. And then, of course, there are all the things that we can do in the mobile world that don't make a lot of sense in the stationary world and those are all the new services.

Industry Standards

On a network level there will continue to be warring standards. 3G does not bring total convergence, although it looks like some TDMA players are going to switch over to GSM – probably a good move. I think on the level of page description, conceptually of course we're great believers in XML. The challenge is getting there, so we have HTML, GHTML, WML and legacy data.

I think over time, yes, there are going to be better standards that have mobile devices in mind. The challenge lies in the fact that we can't wait for them. It will take time for that to happen and that will make all our lives easier. Having said that, we're still going to see a variety of devices with different capabilities, different screen sizes, and different color depths because there are trade-offs. Fortunately there are standards in things like mail already.

Consumer Use

I believe that RIM has done a good job at doing instant email very, very well, and we have incredible respect for the folks there. They recognize that there are limitations for the networks we're running on today and to some extent there always will be. We're finding out that with 3G you've got 384K bandwidth if you're standing pretty close to the tower and there aren't 50 people around you, so you have to know how to deliver services that people love given the limitations. We are great believers that much of the future access to the wireless Internet will actually happen over a Bluetooth access point and other access points that may be in buildings – think about where you spend your day, a lot of it is actually near one of those things.

As far as input, we're going to see a variety of devices. Some devices support both keyboard and tablet-based products. Sharp in Japan has a unit that does both, it has this kind of sliding door on it so you can either use the keyboard device or a tablet. I think people are underestimating the importance of some of the cool new devices we're going to see, and how that's going to make a big difference to people. Why? Because it's what they carry. Look what the Palm 5 did for the Palm business: people said "Hey, this is beautiful! Wow, now when I take this out of my pocket I'm not going to look like a geek – I'm going to look cool." Look at it this way: most companies have not been able to dictate what types of devices their workers use. Imagine asking people at these enterprise conferences, "Okay, how many of you will pay for a cell phone for your workers," and loads of people raise their hand. Then if you ask, "How many of you tell your employees this is the model you have to buy," very few of them raise their hands, because it's like the pen that you carry and who is going to tell you that you cannot carry the pen you want to carry? No one. There's this personal aspect of this business tool. These are knowledge workers and these things are as much an expression of their personalities as they are business tools and we can never lose sight of that so being able to support a variety of them is important.

Keys to Successful Wireless Devices

Success depends on the economic model for one thing. It's tough to push if they're paying by the amount of content, for example. It definitely makes sense to push some things, but the user has to have control over it. I get over 100 emails a day, and I might not want all those pushed to me even if it's free, because it's never really free. Data does take power. The longer you're on your cell phone the more the battery goes down. Besides, I may not want to have to scroll through all those on a smaller device so we think it's important to provide for push services but also to give the user control over it. In the case of the network we're on today, you have to request it. Once the mail is there you can manipulate it the way you like because it's not a browser-based mail client. If you're on a DSL line, browsing is fine for your mail but if you're on a wireless pipe it really isn't, so having a client server architecture where there's intelligence on the client is important.

We believe that some of the richer services can be pushed and some can be pulled but the more important goal is to cache the right things locally so the user has the right kind of experience. If the user doesn't have the right kind of experience they will not use it and the success of that is in the interface.

The Integration of Voice and Wireless

It's an interesting topic, and I think it's multi mode: if I'm driving down the road I better be able to have a lot of voice interactivity because I don't want to run into a tree. On the other hand, in Tokyo this notion of being rude on your cell phone is becoming a big thing. You'll go into hotels and you'll see signs in the lobby saying please don't use your mobile phone. You'll go on the subway and see signs that say please do not talk on your mobile phone. Guess what they're doing, they're doing i-Mode text entry, so that's one thing to think about. There are many situations where I would rather interact through text entry and reading than through voice, so the reality is one size does not fit all. People will ask what's the mode I'm in, what makes the most sense, and what am I comfortable with?

Also, there's a big difference between command and control voice recognition and natural language recognition, which is still not there. I think people are going to have more device choices and there will be places where voice makes lots of sense and places where it may not.

Room for Innovation

I think there are two extremes out there. You have people who say, "Oh, it's the Internet. We'll treat it like an extension of the PC." But the devices have smaller screens and are probably connected over a thin pipe, and there are latency issues so that probably doesn't make total sense. Then there are people saying that networks are really bad and we have to do all these things and we'll never get there. So there's a lot of opportunity for middle-ware rendering techniques. Users hate to enter data more than once, so the question is how do I give intelligence to the transactions that happen on these devices so the user is really just directly entering them rather than having to do lots of graffiti or typing? Users frankly don't want to do either of those, so there are a lot of opportunities there.

Broadly, in the area of software we're starting to see things that do a better job of browsing on small devices while still taking into account there are different kinds of devices. I think the whole notion of location and community is important, gaming may be very important, being able to create your own community of friends, knowing who's on if you want to be seen, knowing where they are if they want to be seen – there are a lot of interesting opportunities there. Devices that have a low power, high quality, very thin screen will help to create an environment that will be night and day to the devices we have today. If we have much smaller, easier to read devices, we'll be willing to do more.

The lower power processors we're seeing are important because it's all about battery life and battery life is about the battery technology and size. I have to worry about power; batteries have not been progressing as quickly, they're very incremental technology. They've been getting smaller, and there are lots of things that are improving about them, but the improvements are incremental.

The Ultimate Handheld Device Is…

It would have a very thin color data pad that has a plastic LCD and digitizer so that if I sat on it I wouldn't kill it, so I could truly throw it in my pocket without worrying about it. It would have Bluetooth technology connected to my very small, sexy world band phone and it would work with the phone anywhere within 25-30 feet. I could have the phone in my briefcase or in my pocket and they would just interoperate seamlessly. When they're together they would work together flawlessly. And here's the key, a phone does what it does very well, it's optimized for interacting on that voice network, dialing numbers and all that, even four-year-olds can use it. A data pad or data-centric device works in a different way, and the challenge in combining the two has always been ergonomics not technology. So my ideal is two optimized devices that are very thin and small and I carry wherever I want. When I don't want to carry one it's just fine and I get an even smaller device but when they're together they work together.

Wireless Worldwide

Clearly we all know that the Japanese are way ahead on the data side and I think that's been very interesting. For one thing they have a standard dominant countrywide network they've been able to leverage. I think also to some extent i-Mode is the Internet in Japan, so the reference point is different. Of course, they will be the first with third-generation networks, so I think they're going to continue to be ahead. Having said that, I think it's very hard to directly transplant the Japanese model elsewhere. Historically, you can't just take U.S. products and drop them directly into Japan, and vice versa, so there has to be some rethinking.

I think Europe is ahead in their roll out. They already allocated the spectrum for the networks, and they know where the spectrum is coming from. It's expensive but they know where it is. The difference is they've been very voice-centric. I'm not sure they're ahead in data. I think the U.S. has actually done a better job of deploying some of the data applications. In the U.S. a lot of data applications are commercial, more so than in other places to date. The problem in the U.S. is we have these proprietary data networks, and on the cellular side we have spectrum issues and geography issues, and we're more challenged on a network roll out. Because we are more data-centric, or at least have more of a balance between voice and data, we have a much better position to potentially leverage the Internet in wireless data services.

The Future of Wireless

Clearly we've seen consolidation on the network side, and I think we'll continue to see that. On the data side this is all very new, and I think we'll continue to see lots of new companies as we always do when there are new technologies and new market opportunities. This will happen because this is a different business than the classic voice business. Think about who provides the content on the voice network. The end user, thank you very much, we provide the content ourselves. I think you're going to see new companies partner with established companies to do these things, and I think that's going to be a pretty prevalent model.

Wireless Winners

First, you have to provide a set of services that people are willing to pay for, so it's got to be truly valuable to them – you have to get the value proposition right. It has to be compelling, it has to be easy to use, they have to really bring value to the user because users are much more particular about what they actually carry on their person than what they have at home, so this has got to be the right stuff.

Next, you have to have great partnerships and alliances. None of us are going to be able to do this on our own. Some companies already control certain points of information for people. For example, AOL has the world's largest email service. Do you think people might want to get to that? You better believe it. Microsoft controls the vast majority of the enterprise email platform and it's growing every day. Do you think you might have to give people access to that? You also have to be able to work on multiple cool devices; you can't say I'm only going to do Palms, because there are going to be other great things out there. Microsoft is going to be a very important player in this space and you better be working closely to help those people for whom it's important to get that stuff, because not only are they going to have great devices based on their system but, frankly, they also own the Exchange and it's going to be important in this space.

Inside the Minds

Patrick McVeigh is Chairman and Chief Executive Officer of OmniSky, Inc. Previously, McVeigh was the Vice President of Worldwide Sales and Business Development at 3Com's Palm Computing unit, and was part of the original management team who transformed this small venture into a market leader with sales in excess of 4 million units. He formed key alliances and partnerships with industry leaders such as IBM, Symbol Technologies, SAP, Oracle, and Lotus. As Vice President of Sales and Marketing for Knowledge Adventure, McVeigh oversaw the development and launch of the 'Jumpstart' series, the number one line of educational software in the industry. Prior to this, he held a number of senior sales and marketing positions at Apple Computer, where he was responsible for the development and launch of the company's new consumer business, Performa.

SANJOY MALIK
Wireless Challenges
Air2Web
Founder, President and CEO

The Draw of Wireless

I had been working in the mobile space at Dunn & Bradstreet and also at Synchrologic. The opportunity for wireless seemed to loom very large at the beginning of last year, so we decided to go out and try to see if we could make it into a great business. The consumers are there, the market is there, the back-end eBusiness applications are there and the wireless infrastructure is there. There is a lot of investment going on in the infrastructure – in both the wireless technology and the backend eBusiness applications. It seemed like a good opportunity to build a large enough business in this space.

Excitement in Wireless

The most exciting aspect of wireless today is the evolution of the computing paradigm, of how we think about, not only computing, but also applications. It is how businesses connect with the consumer, their employees, and their partners. The whole thing is going through a dramatic change. It's similar to when the Internet was first introduced. The relationship between the consumer and business changed with the Internet, and I think that's happening in an even more dramatic fashion with the wireless sector. Wireless technology provides for the opportunity of interacting at the time and place which is most convenient. In the 4 P's of marketing a product or service – Product, Price, Promotion and Place – wireless essentially makes the "place" factor infinite. This increases the value proposition to the consumer.

The Future of Wireless

For the last 10 years, wireless has been about investment, infrastructure, and getting the consumers to a point where they are ready for wireless to become part of how they do business. The Internet revolution created an abundance of online business applications. Now the devices themselves have evolved to a point where they're able to support more intelligent applications. The infrastructure is there in terms of coverage. Essentially, you can use one wireless device, and still have seamless access across the world. As all of this comes together, you have the big bang of linking wireless technology and the online business applications. Thus, mobile business applications are created.

Consumer Readiness

There are a lot of people, probably 500 million, who are using wireless devices today. That's a huge number of devices that are already out there. Most of them are used as phones. People are use to having these devices with them at all times, sitting inside their pocket, or hanging on their belt, or sitting in their purse. That part of the wireless paradigm has already been accepted and is being used. In terms of the applications, that is something new. These applications are enhancing the utility of the investment people have made in these devices. This type of use is rapidly growing, and it is only going to take a few years for it to settle into the mainstream way in which we do business.

Issues Facing the Wireless Industry

I think that if the 3G infrastructure was fully operational and in place there would be more compelling applications today, but I don't think it's really slowing down the market itself. I strongly believe that the technology and the infrastructure that is there now can be used to create some very compelling applications. Real businesses can start accessing their end-users through this medium today. Therefore, I don't think it's the technology and the infrastructure that's slowing things down. I just think it's a normal evolution of the businesses getting acclimated to this new way of getting their products out to their customers, partners, and employees. This is just going to take some time. Today, without 3G, there are still thousands of UPS customers tracking shipments from mobile devices, and thousands of customers managing their bank accounts from their phones. 3G and GPRS will definitely pave the way for richer applications. However, even if 3G were here today, I don't think it would make a huge amount of difference in terms of market acceptance or user acceptance because consumers' incorporation of these new applications into their daily lives is just beginning.

Popular Applications

I don't believe there is going to be one or two dominant wireless applications. I think this phenomenon is going to be much broader than just having one or two killer applications. It would be like saying there are only one or two main Internet applications. Wireless is just like an electric grid. You plug in a toaster, you plug in a refrigerator, and you plug in the TV. Similarly, you will use the wireless network infrastructure for different kinds of things, whether it's for business, for consumer oriented things, entertainment, media, or security.

The Status and Direction of Wireless

The industry, as such, is at a fairly mature level. The network infrastructure is very robust and is provided by good companies with great geographic coverage. Consumers have access to brand name services so they don't have to deal with unknown players. At the next level, data services are still evolving, but they are being built on a very solid and robust infrastructure. This is where there's a lot of opportunity for innovation and new businesses are moving fairly rapidly into this space to take advantage of the huge investment that has gone into the infrastructure and existing customer base.

U.S. Opportunities Versus the Rest of the World

Opportunities in the U.S. are a little bit different because we started earlier with wireless than the rest of the world.

Therefore, we are encumbered with an abundance of different standards, CDMA, DSM, GDMA, etc. We did not have the luxury of picking one network standard. Europe and some of the rest of the world adopted a more uniform standard, the GSM network. However, the types of applications that Europe and other areas went for were mostly consumer-oriented applications that offered messaging, chat rooms, jokes, horoscopes, and things like that. The U.S. has taken a different path towards wireless applications. I think the path is more business-oriented. Not to say that there won't be consumer applications, but the U.S. is leading the charge with business and e-commerce solutions. That's where I think we will have an advantage over the rest of the world.

I think opportunities in wireless are different in the U.S. I think there's going to be more innovation here because the culture is more entrepreneurial. There's a wider range of eBusiness applications that can be extended to wireless devices. Additionally, there is less control over how an application accesses a wireless network. In the rest of the world, access to the network is controlled by the carriers, and in the U.S., it's less so. It's more of an open playing field. I think you'll see more innovation. Long term, I don't think we'll be at a disadvantage.

Supply and Demand for Wireless Infrastructure

A prime example of a market where there are no licensing costs is in Japan. The Japanese government is giving away the frequencies, so the cost and the economic model associated with using these frequencies and what you can do with them is dramatically different from a country like the U.S. In markets where the frequencies are auctioned off for billions of dollars, the people who have the right to use these frequencies are already encumbered with much more of a capital expense. The economic model, of how you use the bandwidth and the frequencies available, changes considerably.

I think to some extent the expense of building the wireless infrastructure does have some effect, but innovation is extremely important. Achieving an acceptable return-on-investment for these extremely large outlays will require compelling applications that are valuable to the end-users. It is the applications that drive value for the end-users. So, the question becomes how to drive valuable applications. The carriers recognize that an open approach to innovation, an approach that empowers application development across the greatest number of sources, will ultimately result in the most compelling solutions. In turn, the networks will be utilized more frequently, which will benefit the carriers.

Challenges to the Wireless Industry

I think one of the biggest challenges is getting the data services infrastructure scaled higher. This infrastructure is still very shaky. Also, the interfaces to the devices and networks are varied. A single uniform standard may never emerge. However, with or without a standard like XML or HGML, as long as the devices can communicate with one another through applications it really doesn't matter what operating system is in them and what interfaces are required to connect them.

The Wireless Commercial Value

Wireless applications are becoming vehicles for initiating commerce transactions. These applications could be as basic as buying a Coke from a Coke machine or zapping money to your child's cell phone to cover cab fare home in an emergency. Wireless technology increases the opportunity for person-to-person payments and transactions. That's incredible. So, once you start looking at these simple solutions and start adding these up into more complex applications, the opportunities are endless. There are other group applications such as "voting for the player of the week," whereby people inside a stadium are able to interact with one another and immediately see the results on the scoreboard. Wireless devices also become a vehicle for receiving media. A grandmother, visiting the Grand Canyon, could instantly transmit photos of her trip to her grandchildren.

Device Diversity

I think wireless diversity is really very good because the multitude of device types will become tuned to the user's requirements. Devices will take the shape and form of what you want to do with them. For example, you could have one wireless device which lets you listen to the radio, pick your choices of songs or is connected to the Internet, but that's a different kind of device than a PDA. A PDA lets you synchronize calendars across a huge wireless network to other devices. Yet other wireless devices are the GPS tracking systems built into your car and the security collar on your dog which lets you track him if he is lost. As a user you will select the device the best matches your needs, the challenge then moves to the application side. A business will want to provide services to their entire customer base, but how can you build applications that work across the myriad of devices? And how do you optimize those applications for the unique capabilities of individual devices? It becomes impractical to develop multiple versions of an application for each device type. Instead a business needs a platform that answers the one application to many device type challenges.

Government Regulation

Essentially, I think the government can be very helpful if they provide base-level standards, but not get too involved with the innovation or the setting of standards. An example of government regulation is the whole issue of the location business. Today, the technology exists for location services. However, because of privacy concerns by the government, and to some extent those concerns are valid, the carriers and others will not provide location information except for the 911 type services. The government does and can influence the level of innovation in terms of what kinds of things happen and how fast they happen.

Simplifying Interfaces

I think that simpler interfaces among devices will happen. In Japan, people are very, very comfortable with using small screens and limited keyboards for messages. The interfaces will get better in other ways. These devices are getting more specific to what they are meant to deliver in applications. If it's a phone, then the interface is very, very adequate. If you want to use it as a messaging device, that's when you start seeing a problem. The problem arises when you try to apply existing applications to those smaller devices. It's similar to the first television shows; they were simply radio shows on TV. Eventually, everyone learns the ins and outs of the new technology. So, you'll see different form factors and different formats and different applications. The screens will not necessarily get bigger; however, the development of voice and audio based application interfaces bypass the challenges of small screens and keyboards. I think it's unreasonable to expect just one form factor to exist with everything you want to do with wireless.

Wireless Bandwidth

We are still a few years away from a mass-market adoption of broadband wireless. I don't think the networks exist, and even if they did exist it would take awhile for these kinds of technologies to penetrate the mass market. However, we will start seeing some innovative uses of these applications in the near future. We are, I would say, two to four years away from seeing more adoption in the marketplace.

Players in the Wireless Market

Like any other emerging technology and emerging market, venture capitalists make a huge impact. The markets influence the early investors in terms of what they can expect for the risk they are taking. However, investors are excited about the wireless marketplace and the steamroller is moving. This market is the intersection of eBusiness and wireless communications. As important as the VCs are, you simply cannot ignore the influences of existing companies in the wireless and Internet space. There's a huge momentum behind the developments in the mobile arena, and there's no turning back. This market is going to happen, you can probably tweak its path a little bit and maybe slow it or speed it up a little bit. If anything, I think it is a question of how quickly and what particular path the evolution might take, not whether or not it will actually happen.

Winning in Wireless

I think many of the core factors for success in the wireless industry are not inherently different from the factors of success in building any business. It is a question of businesses that are built on solid fundamentals and businesses that take advantage of the opportunities that exist. The opportunity is for people to put out innovative products and services and use the wireless infrastructure to deliver them. However, one has to find customers for these products and services, and they must deliver value to the consumer, thus giving them a compelling need to buy them.

Malik has more than 16 years of experience in the software development industry. Before founding Air2Web, he started Synchrologic, Inc.-a leading developer of Internet-based mobile computing software. As founder and President, he was responsible for raising venture capital, hiring a successful management team and establishing partnerships with key industry leaders. Prior to founding Synchrologic, Malik served as Director of Development and Program Management at Sales Technologies and held several engineering positions at Intergraph. Malik earned dual master's degrees in Computer Sciences and Engineering from the University of Florida, as well as a bachelor of science degree in Engineering from IIT Delhi.

PAUL SETHY
The High Costs of Wireless
AirPrime
Founder & Chairman

Background Information

I'm a local kid from Silicon Valley. I've spent 21 years in high technology, primarily on the communications side and have been most active in the data networking part of communications, and with wireless in the last several years. I've worked with many different flavors of wireless technology, adapting different platforms for different world markets on a variety of wireless networks. In '96 I observed the PCS auctions that were occurring in the U.S. market. The World Trade Organization was encouraging PCS implementations as a principal part of the push for deregulation in worldwide telecommunications. That became very interesting to me, because if every country in the world was clearing out frequency for a PCS system, a personal communication system for voice, video and data, it meant that we had the possibility of a worldwide Internet backbone based on that infrastructure. What was most intriguing to me was that the infrastructure was being built out first for voice. The cost of that which is in the many tens of billions of dollars per country could be leveraged for data as well as voice with just an incremental upgrade to the infrastructure.

The Evolution of Wireless

The Wireless Industry

Wireless has been around for a long time, since the invention of the radio. I think we've seen a migration over the last 20 years from wireless that was predominantly used for military, industrial, scientific, and medical purposes, to wireless technologies now being adopted at much lower cost points in the commercial and consumer world. We started back in the early 1980's with primarily wireline technologies, whether it was twisted pair for telephone services or cabling for Ethernet and token ring services. Now we're migrating to the point where there is an explosion in transferring telecommunication and computing devices onto complete wireless systems. Our focus at Air Prime is on providing wireless solutions for computing and networking devices that are low cost and easily adopted by end users. The key factor here is cost. We are able to leverage PCS infrastructure networks that are currently built out and take advantage of the significantly decreasing cost in components for cellular devices. As cellular shipments have gone up over the last 15 years, the cost of components has come down dramatically, and now we're able to leverage those cost points in terms of designing cost-effective products for the data side of the market.

The Benefits of Wireless Technology

There are many different forms of wireless microwave technologies used in radio, television, satellite, local area network and wide area networks. If we're specifically talking about the niche of the market that we play in, which is cellular wireless technology, you have three competing standards out there, GSM, which has the largest market share, TDMA, and then CDMA, which is the fastest growing sector in cellular. All of these technologies are migrating toward one or more flavors of what we call third-generation or 3G technology. The big winners are the developing countries of the world where they're leapfrogging the implementation of nationwide communications systems based on these new technologies. It would be cost prohibitive to spend the number of man years in implementing wireline solutions. Leapfrogging to complete wireless systems makes the most sense. China is the premier example of that, but this is going on throughout the world. Prior to starting Air Prime, I was at the Hewlett Packard division of VeriFone, the worldwide leader in the manufacturing of credit card transaction devices. One of the biggest problems for the credit card industry is that the biggest open markets for credit cards are developing countries, especially with the populations of China and India. But, most of those devices were built to run on standard twisted pier wiring systems. By developing systems for devices other than laptops and PDAs and Internet appliances, whether it's test equipment or credit card transaction readers or metering and monitoring equipment, telemetry and telematics equipment or pre-paid disposable phones, it allows us to leverage wireless capabilities, especially if you can adopt them into various platforms at a low enough cost.

Developing the Wireless Space

When I sat down to put together the business plan for Air Prime I wanted to focus on what I viewed as a multi-billion dollar market opportunity, not just a small niche of the industry. With all of the standards moving toward 3G, third-generation cellular, and migrating toward a common denominator of technology, CDMA or wide band CDMA, this is going to allow PCS infrastructures worldwide to become the reality of what was a dream just years ago: a universal wireless system for the world, not just for voice but for data and video applications as well. Within this space there are many types of businesses that will succeed, carriers like Sprint PCS or Verizon or Telstron in Australia that are the backbone of providing nationwide subscription services. You also have clear winners in the equipment space, whether it's for base station equipment or cards that will upgrade these base stations for future services, and with the device manufacturers like ourselves that are linked in more with the subscriber end of the technology.

There are also tremendous winners in the server marketplace. If I can draw an analogy here from my 3Com days, I remember Bob Metcalfe saying there eventually would be dozens and dozens of companies building Ethernet cards in competition with 3Com. In fact, this is what happened. Margins thinned out over time and many businesses went under because it became too competitive. So what strategy would preserve 3Com's leadership position? One way to maintain your margins was to create links between an Ethernet network interface card and your servers, and eventually between the Ethernet and the wiring closet equipment. That allowed a company like 3Com to become a systems solution center for customers. If you really wanted to take full advantage of their Ethernet cards in the desktop, you bought all of the equipment, the wiring closet equipment plus the Ethernet cards from them. If you bought them from another provider you were not leveraging the full capabilities within the system. Similarly in the wireless world, you're creating wireless modems that will now be prevalent in millions of devices. They are going to be dependent upon application servers and server farms that are either located at the carriers or managed by somebody else for the carriers. The Internet content providers will also have influence on those wireless devices. So to the extent we can create hooks between the wireless devices and the server forms, we see some tremendous opportunities emerging.

What kind of services will be offered? Location services, emergency 911 services, pre-paid phone services, all kinds of enterprise applications as well as just standard connections to the Internet. You could even see the major television and entertainment studios getting involved in this realm as well. I believe you are going to see winners in all of these areas.

Lastly, of key focus to the current venture capital environment are the software opportunities in wireless, whether it is leveraging the WAP protocol, or leveraging the Internet protocol. One of the key reasons I focused on CDMA is that it is an IP-centric technology from the ground up. That means that all of the base band processors have the full IP protocol stack already on the chip and we can leverage that to tie in and link into the worldwide Internet protocol system. So we're at the very embryonic stage of this market taking off. Many analysts and many of the corporations that are planning future products for laptops, PDAs, Internet appliances, and the migration of cell phones into various types of devices, are forecasting the extension of wireless to millions of users who previously did not have access to any information network.

The Importance of Capital

If you look at it from a global picture venture capital has not been that important, because wireless has been almost completely dominated by the multi-billion dollar companies around the world. Therefore, it's been very hard for a small startup company to suddenly be building products for the base station environment of cellular wireless when it's dominated by Lucent, Nortel, Motorola, Ericsson, Samsung, and companies like that. In other areas of technology, let's say CDMA, the technology's been controlled primarily by a Qualcommm company that effectively has a monopoly in this space much like a Microsoft or an Intel. So there have been many strong barriers to entry for small startup companies getting off the ground in wireless. Major success stories in the past two decades are few and far between. MCI, Qualcommm, McCow are examples of some of the successes and all faced enormous uphill battles in establishing their leadership positions. There are many greater opportunities on the software side than on the hardware side, but hardware is where the big revenues are. In the Price Waterhouse Cooper quarterly venture capital survey, the number of startups in the wireless arena, each quarter are usually one, two, or three wireless startups getting off the ground, most of them on the software side and just a handful every year in the hardware or a combination of hardware and software, so it is a difficult place to break into. But I think that you see a lot of the focus today in the software arena. It is the easiest environment for a startup company to break into and attract venture capital money. That is where there is the most intense venture capital interest, the least barriers to entry, and billion-dollar corporations that can become immediate customers of these technologies.

The Effect of the Market on Startups

Companies are jumping the gun in terms of accessing the public markets when there is sufficient private capital available to fund these opportunities to a more mature stage. That's why you see valuations that are lower than people were expecting, and many of these stocks are trading either just above issue or slightly below.

You also have other companies in the wireless Internet service provider space that I think are also being held back for a few reasons. One is that they are bringing in very little or modest revenue compared to the cash flow going out to build their companies. One thing that I fear, especially with Verizon and Sprint and AT&T and many of the major carriers involved in offering wireless data services, is that these smaller firms that have now gone public are beginning to look like the dot.com companies. They're spending bucket loads amount of money on advertising and PR to attract subscribers at very high per subscriber costs and not bringing in a sufficient amount of revenue to really look like they have a good business model. They could be crushed by the major carriers once they become involved.

I'm going to give you one other example, Metro Com which is very well known for its Ricochet wireless devices. However, the company has been losing money every single quarter for five or six years. They're spending about $5 or $6, of their capital, on infrastructure for every $1 that they bring in in revenue from subscribers. In fact, in at least two quarters in a row early this year, the number of subscribers fell instead of increasing. How long can you continue on a business model like that? That is of concern to me, which is one reason why AirPrime decided to focus on the device side of the industry where there's very solid revenue and leverage a built-out infrastructure. It's extremely strong revenue growth right off the bat, very high demand, we break even in the second year of business, and there's very strong positive cash flow by the end of the third year.

Successful Startups

I certainly think that there is an environment right now on Wall Street and in the venture capital community that whether you're a new venture getting off the ground or an existing one reaching toward some maturity level, you have to show a business model that is going to get you to revenue and profitability at the earliest point in time. It's not just having revenue either. It is having strong sustainable growth over a period of time. I think people are much more focused on market share the last couple of years. You can take a look at the Internet content type companies or e-commerce companies. Many them were copycat companies, and the PetStore.com type ventures. It was like there was one a week getting off the ground for an entire quarter in the venture community, and those are easily replicated businesses. Market share becomes diluted very quickly if there are several successful companies, or you're going to end up with one winner out of the whole group and it's a crapshoot. I think you have to be able to show customer demand and that you have a good shot at becoming either the number one or number two player in your industry.

Worldwide Wireless

It depends on what technology and what area you're focused on. If you look at cellular technology, I believe that the existing market share leaders in the hardware area will principally come out of the U.S. markets or from Asia. The U.S. seems to have a very strong set of players in base station equipment manufacturing, although there are others like Ericsson in Europe that are successful too, and Samsung over in Korea. In terms of handsets I think you really have a worldwide distribution of companies: Samsung, Hyundai, all emanating out of Korea, companies like Motorola in the United States, Nokia and Ericsson in Europe. So for handsets it seems to be distributed on a more equal basis around the world. For base stations it's primarily the U.S. with some going to Asia and Europe. For modem manufacturing it's primarily going to be the U.S. and Asia, and for software I think Europe is a very clear winner.

It's very exciting to see all of the entrepreneurial companies getting off the ground throughout Europe that are application developers and leveraging different wireless protocols. I believe that many of those companies will make wonderful acquisition opportunities, because they are not being capitalized or valued at the same levels of wireless companies in the U.S. market. You're able to buy them at a discount to what you would purchase a similar company in the U.S. Again, in Europe I think the focus has shifted more to software because there are even higher barriers in the European markets to get involved in hardware manufacturing. I don't believe that the Asian companies will be much of a factor in the host software area, at least not in the next few years. That seems to be their one weak point. And in the United States we have tremendous opportunities, and it's for several reasons. One, I think we have the clear edge in talent when it comes to leveraging the Internet protocol, and that will be the key to all of these future wireless technologies moving forward. So Silicon Valley should certainly be the focal point of that. Two, I think people have a little bit more opportunity to enter the hardware businesses not only because of the availability of capital, but because the barriers to entry are a little bit lower as well.

Wireless solutions today are chiefly focused on cellular handsets, in the near future moving to computing devices like PDAs, but one of the most vigorous areas of venture capital investment over the last two or three years has been for fixed wireless services on different microwave frequencies, whether it was for unlicensed or a licensed frequency. One of the most exciting areas of development where I see opportunity in the wireless marketplace is in solving this problem. We're seeing various Internet and data focused solutions like DSL to the home or business, fiber to the curb, and specific microwave services that accomplish that last mile or last few miles solution. The data rates on cellular technology are moving rapidly from 14.4 currently to 144kb this year, and in 2002 the rollout starts for IXEV, which will offer high data rate technology at a megabit or more. For example, CDMA is 2.4 megabits per second, and some of the European technologies are being adopted under GPRS at 2 megabits per second. This is an immense revolution that's going on in a very compressed period of time to go from 14.4 in the year 2000 to suddenly a megabit or more in 2002, and I think this is going to solve a lot of the last mile solutions that people have been looking for in data services with multiple options covering voice, video and data. There will be tremendous startup opportunities ignited by these changes.

Factors Affecting the Industry

You're going to see a couple of different effects from the shortage of wireless frequencies and licensing costs here. One is on the basis of cost. Because of limited spectrum availability, I think the carriers are going to feel a little bit more liberated to charge more or as much as they can, as demand exceeds supply or availability of service. Carriers will be competing for that available spectrum.

Licensing costs are another barrier to entry, which is why you don't see too many startups successfully obtaining licenses and then converting that into an actual business. You have seen startups or limited partnerships bid on licenses and then sell them in the open market to some of the big players. But I do feel encouraged by the FCC and some of the executive orders of the President to clear out frequencies that are currently used by the military, to expand the spectrum for PCS by quite a bit, and to open up other frequencies as well. In that regard, one interesting development that you may see is that today we have CDMA primarily in the cellular frequencies either at 1.9 gigahertz or in the 800 to 900 megahertz frequency. You will probably start seeing other frequencies adopting CDMA cellular technologies.

The Cost of Wireless Infrastructure

There are many different types of wireless technology under development. Array Com is another example right here in Santa Clara, a company started by the developer of the first cellular phone at Motorola. While all of them are interesting technologies and can offer high speed capability at some point, I believe that the cost of building out the infrastructure is just too high and in many cases irrecoverable, which is why I believe that people who are leveraging current cellular infrastructures are going to be the ones that gain the most.

Let me give you another analogy in that respect. If you go back 15 years to Ethernet in the middle 1980's, it was not apparent that Ethernet was going to be the big winner. There were token ring systems, different types of broadband systems being offered, and everybody had their own flavor of networking technology and sets of protocols that they were trying to get adopted into standards, or they were offering some proprietary networking standard. I think what pushed Ethernet beyond the pack was the breakthrough of getting the technology to work on twisted pair. Once that was achieved, it became relatively feasible to leverage the twisted pair wiring systems that were already in place in all of the commercial buildings across the country and around the world. If you could walk into a building, install some wiring closet equipment and plug a wire into the wall to your desktop you were leveraging infrastructure rather than having to build it all out, and the same thing is occurring in wireless today. There are many different flavors of wireless, everybody trying to build their own infrastructures. I think the real breakthrough occurring now is that we've been able to solve the problem of how to offer higher data rates over cellular infrastructures that are already being built out. For example, in the U.S. we have spent close to $100 billion in the cost of licenses and building out the PCS infrastructure. Who in their right mind would want to recreate that all over again, when you now have ubiquitous, universal, geographic coverage over every major metropolitan area, in addition to the continuing tier two and tier three build outs to all the suburban and rural areas.

So I think cost of infrastructure is a very important question in how you develop any successful business model. There are niches of the market where it makes sense to build out your own infrastructure and where you can get a return: for example public utilities or the military, private networks where you want ultimate security and integrity in your network, and for major corporations that want to put in private networks where security is of utmost importance. I think you will see certain microwave technologies succeed where the cost of building up infrastructure is worth it.

Short Message Service

SMS has been very successful over in Europe. The expansion of the number of messages per month in Europe went from a very small number per month to 10 million and then 100 million per month, and it's rising dramatically. I'm not sure whether SMS is going to be successful in the North American markets. I think that we are moving very quickly toward the point where we're going to have devices that have the Internet protocol support on them, and new forms of messaging services will exist on the infrastructure. I look at SMS as something that occurred in the infancy stage on a cellular network in Europe at very low data rates, but as we move to PDA and Internet appliances companies bringing out sophisticated messages and messaging systems it is going to be very different.

Government Regulation

The U.S. is criticized frequently for not promoting common technology standards across our country, which has limited our ability to take advantage of new applications and services such as SMS over in Europe or i-Mode in Japan. But our market is a deregulated market. We no longer live in a MaBell only world. The FCC and Congress, for the most part, are encouraging competition. That means a lot of different flavors of technology in our market that are competing for market share or leading edge dominance in the marketplace. I do not anticipate a shift from that strategy, but I do believe that the FCC is being quite visionary in thinking about how the entire world ends up with a common set of frequencies or a common technology that is adopted, and the World Trade Organization also is being very progressive in that manner. So to the extent that CDMA technology is the best technology in the world to adopt, the FCC, The World Trade Organization, and all of our trade negotiators have really put their political muscle behind trying to see that CDMA technology is successfully adopted in other countries around the world. When it came to negotiating with China, for example, our government really stood behind Qualcommm in the negotiating sessions with the Chinese to encourage CDMA to be adopted above competing technologies from Europe and from within Asia too. So domestically I think it's going one way toward greater competition, and internationally I think we're playing a very strong role in trying to push U.S.-sponsored technology.

I think that the U.S. and our Congress need to realize that 3G is the future of world communications and that what may have started out as a pilot system with limited frequency available for PCS is going to be completely saturated within a matter of years. We need to plan right now for broader spectrum availability or different sets of spectrum set aside for these types of services. The U.S. can play a very important part in aggressively opening up frequency. I read through former President Bill Clinton's executive order that he put out last fall, encouraging the opening of more spectrum and shifting spectrum away from areas where the military currently has entitlements. The key reason, in his opinion, was that this would open up not only more competition, but it would encourage the development of more startups and entrepreneurial ventures in the U.S. market. If we do not open up more frequency to foster the development of more business opportunities, we're going to miss out on a key economic engine for our country's future where we could be a driving force worldwide.

The Wireless Industry

Paul Sethy possesses more than 20 years of business experience in technology, having worked for companies including Kodak/Verbatim, Xerox, 3Com, and Hewlett-Packard/VeriFone. An expert in networking and communications technology, Paul is also a businessman with a keen eye for integrating all aspects of growing and managing a business. He has managed the introduction of several premier product lines in the networking and telecom industries, ensuring their timely progression from engineering concept to more than $100 million in revenue. Throughout his career, Paul has built OEM relationships with key strategic vendors while supporting sales organizations for both direct and distributor sales in the networking and communications industry. A Silicon Valley native, Paul attended UC Berkeley where he majored in Economics and Business Administration.

REZA AHY
Developing Areas of Wireless
Aperto Networks
President and CEO

The Future of Wireless

The wireless industry in general has three flavors. The first variety is narrowband mobile devices, and you see a tremendous bit of growth in those areas inclusive of PDAs, handhelds and mobile cellular, voice and data combined. The second is going be wideband portable and quasi-stationary applications such as wireless LAN and 3G, third-generation cellular devices which again combine data and voice. The most exciting thing is the third variety and that's what Aperto Networks is focused on. That is fixed broadband wireless, and by broadband I mean multi-megabit services and applications running on stationary wireless platforms for multiple services. That's what I see as the most exciting branch of the wireless industry as a whole and one that truly is a market in search of a solution. The shortcomings and the huge service voids left behind by DSL and cable modem for the mass volume broadband access is being addressed by wireless broadband. That is extremely exciting in the sense that the fixed wireless industry has never before had the ability to fulfill the needs of tens of millions of potential broadband users worldwide in a way that the wireline industry cannot accomplish alone.

The Benefits of Wireless

Wireless broadband technology will benefit end user consumers and small-to-medium businesses in terms of the ability to be significantly more efficient in carrying out their day-to-day business and normal life. The service providers will benefit because it enables very rapid service delivery and supports substantially different types of services, applications, offerings, and different types of revenue models. And thirdly, equipment manufacturers such as ourselves and the corresponding system integrators will benefit because of this enormous need globally for a new infrastructure that is not only capable of voice, such as copper line infrastructure, but also multi- services (data, voice, and video) in the years to come.

Meeting Public Expectations

I believe broadband wireless, done in the right manner, solves very significant problems in the marketplace for the public. Specifically, today the most significant problem is lack of broadband availability to millions of locations, meaning you may not be able to get DSL or cable modem access in many houses or small business sites. In my house, I can get neither of them, and in fact I cannot get any of the other auxiliary types of solutions, like fiber to the home. For a significant percentage of the U.S. consumer market, the only thing the consumer is left with is the analog modem, which is very low speed and certainly not scalable to the upper reaches of broadband. As a result, the public would benefit enormously by having a true broadband solution available, that's challenge number one, and that's the merit of the fixed wireless broadband access solution.

One way to connect the public to the Internet is direct connection, meaning basically a laptop in an unstructured environment with no gateway around, and clearly that is addressed by the second wireless variety I mentioned earlier. Companies working in the 3G space for portable devices would be able to deliver this. But the more practical solution, in my opinion, is that of combining wireless LANs with broadband access, meaning portables can connect to a gateway wirelessly, and through the gateway – whether it is DSL, cable modem, or broadband wireless – they have connectivity at very high speed to the wireline network.

A Path to Profitability

Profitability is very important for wireless companies. Clearly if you're building a company as a business, it's a very different proposition than if you're building an R & D shop for future acquisition. We are focused very much on revenue and profitability. Clearly that cannot be achieved in one step, and there are phases that a company like us will go through in terms of milestones: early stage and development phase, marching toward alpha stage, beta stage and revenue phase of the company, first customer shipped and then steadily upwards in terms of revenue growth, leading to profitability and down the line, the public offering.

For any wireless company, it is important to be focused on a public offering because that allows us to streamline and become leaner in terms of engineering, marketing, sales and across the board toward demanding of ourselves very crisp and clear results. This is essential to compete with the best of breed players in the marketplace, both against public and private company leaders.

Worldwide Wireless

Specifically, the U.S. is very unique in the sense that the variety of fixed network infrastructures is further along than elsewhere in the world. For the rest of the world, the range of wireline infrastructures is simply not in place. Even in Japan or Western Europe, the cable infrastructure is substantially smaller as compared to the U.S. In 90 percent of the world, cable infrastructure simply does not exist.

We are very active in the U.S., northwestern Europe, Japan, Korea, and a couple of other countries in Asia where fixed wireless can offer a tremendous boost in making broadband accessible to existing user demand. We're predominantly focused on the developed world, but that is not to say that the opportunity does not exist elsewhere. In fact, globally speaking, in the rest of the world the opportunity is huge because the lack of any infrastructure is very high. But we have chosen to focus on developed countries because we can develop a much more predictable model and significantly higher visibility in terms of a business plan. As time elapses, however, and through our partners, we will address other market opportunities outside these areas that I mentioned.

The U.S., certainly, with the pinnacle of broadband wireless access demand, will be a leader in wireless technologies. Here, the issue of availability is a major problem, due to the fact that DSL is very painful to provision, both for consumers and for service providers. There is a market in search of a solution, and if a wireless alternative exists that can alleviate this provisioning pain, millions will buy it. The dynamics of the European market, with the 500-year-old streets and houses and offices where digging trenches is even more of a problem, makes broadband wireless even more attractive. In Japan or Korea, when you look at the logistics of the density and distribution of the connectivity solutions, broadband wireless has yet another set of dynamics that makes it extremely attractive. All in all, we believe that the developed countries will be leading the pack, enabling the rest of the world.

Mainstream Wireless

GPRS is available today in parts of the world and GSM 2 ½ will also make some data, be it narrow band or quasi-wide band, available for mobile users. 3G has the promise of bringing higher-speed convergence applications to the mobile, but the jury's still out on whether that will be the killer application. In other words, whether there is a need in having a very high-speed connectivity while you're driving your car 80 miles an hour is debatable. It is my opinion that the 2 ½ type of generation will address a significant aspect of the mobile convergence or multi services to a large extent. I have serious doubts about 3G as a solution and the existence of the market for 3G in the U.S.

The Cost of Building the Wireless Infrastructure

When you refer to high expense infrastructure, traditionally in wireless this refers to the mobile infrastructure, where service providers pay the upfront millions, if not billions, in terms of capital investment for the mobile user. Let me give you an example. Before you can use your cell phone, the whole infrastructure has to be in place for you to go from one tower to another tower to another while you're roaming around. That is very different from fixed broadband wireless. In fixed broadband wireless, service providers can focus on one pocket of coverage at a time, one business – and address that with a backhaul connectivity and you're done. It's a pay-as-you-grow business model, which makes it extremely attractive for providers because they can focus on the most lucrative aspects of their markets with the segment or a pocket where they have users already identified. They can put up a base station and get the services up and running, generating revenue immediately without having to spend enormously upfront in terms of pre-deploying the infrastructure everywhere. Fixed broadband wireless is a pocket-by-pocket capture and a fundamentally different business model as compared to mobile wireless infrastructure. As a result it makes it a more early-ROI oriented business and revenue model for the service providers.

Issues Facing the Wireless Industry

Clearly the need for spectrum is always there, and higher demand for more and more spectrum is going to continue for a long time. Having said that, however, a number of services are running very successfully today in the U.S. and across the globe in terms of the cellular PCS and mobile type of applications, for voice in particular and narrowband data. As for the demand for higher-speed type of services, again the jury's out in terms of whether you really need a mega-bit service while you're driving. My opinion is that you don't need that. Look at the common sense aspect of the application: if you're checking your email you don't need a 1 mega-bit pipe, you don't even need a few hundred kb of pipe; you basically need a narrowband or quasi-wide band. As a result again, the spectrum that is allocated for 2 ½ generation is adequate for the short term. Over the longer term there is going to be a need for higher amounts of spectrum, but I think that needs to be examined carefully for the mobile applications in terms of how they complement portable and fixed broadband wireless applications. In other words, a very holistic approach to a rational allocation of spectrum resources to the appropriate demand in the marketplace is necessary. That means that for fixed broadband where you really need tremendous amounts of spectrum, that should be allocated according, for narrow-band mobile, the existing spectrum and some additional spectrum should be allocated, and clearly wireless LAN there is already spectrum available in terms of the 2.4 GHz and 5 GHz ISM bands. As the demand grows, the FCC might consider additional spectrum to be allocated.

Government Regulation

The angle of the U.S. government will be from a regulatory perspective. The allocation of spectrum is the most significant impact they can have in terms of standards. Specifically in wireless LAN, 2.4 GHz, the FCC moved to release the 5.2 band (5.1-5.25 GHz band) for indoor wireless LAN which has tremendous impact both on the equipment provider and on the service provider side to enable significant areas of economy and to bring to fruition a lot of the solutions. I believe the same thing will happen in the access area and specifically broadband wireless access. There is a tremendous need in this country in terms of the consumer and the enhancement of effectiveness and efficiency of carrying out business on a day-to-day basis based on availability of broadband pipes.

Short Message Service

I do have some skepticism with respect to whether 3G is an appropriate technology, at least in the short term for the U.S., given that the service providers have already spent billions of dollars in terms of 2G and 2 ½ G, and they're just about ready to generate some revenue in these fronts. We already have SMS and voice access with these current systems. SMS is proven in terms of market viability – this puts a question mark in terms of whether 3G is needed in the U.S.

Advice for Startups

Wireless is a very difficult area of technology, and fixed broadband wireless is even more difficult. In general, my advice for any startup, wireless or otherwise, but in particular for wireless, is the need to focus on results and narrow down a solution in the marketplace. It is a classic mistake to try to do too much as a startup, but one can also fail miserably by trying to do too little. The biggest challenge for a startup is to make sure you're focusing on your core value and being checked by the marketplace – meaning you're not designing a technology for the technology's sake but rather a solution for the market and solving a customer's problem. You must also have a tight focus but simultaneously a broad vision with key emphasis on execution, execution, and execution.

On Leadership

I moved through the ranks. I started my career as an engineer and I moved through the management ranks in marketing and business development, engineering, and general management, so that has been a tremendous experience. Having an in-depth and broad technology understanding helps me enormously in terms of day-to-day effectiveness. Having the business skills to understand what truly makes or breaks a solution out there in the marketplace, and building solutions, not technologies, for our customers has helped me enormously in terms of ability to distinguish between different aspects of the decision making on a day-to-day basis.

Overcoming Obstacles

The Wireless Industry

Everybody goes through obstacles in their career. The merit of an obstacle is to provide an opportunity for all of us to learn. I regard them as positive, and focusing on solving them has made me a better person and more capable than I was prior to that experience

Prior to founding Aperto Networks, Dr. Ahy held executive and technical senior management positions with Harris Corporation, Varian Research Center and RadioLAN, focused on businesses and products in broadband wireless & high-speed optical communications systems. Dr. Ahy earned his BSEE and MSEE from the University of California, San Diego and his Ph.D.EE from Stanford University.

Inside the Minds

MARTIN COOPER
The Real Potential for Wireless
Arraycomm
Chairman and CEO

My Background & The Wireless History

I worked at Motorola and I was there for some 29 years starting as a research engineer. When we developed the first cellular phone I was running a division of Motorola that managed all of the radio/telephone businesses. Previous to that I started the radio paging business – the high Capacity Paging business. I created the concept of trunking in dispatch two-way radio that ultimately became the SMRS industry, Special Mobile Radio Services, which was the first use of trunked radio channels in radiotelephone. In the late 1960's AT&T, proposed to the FCC that the FCC allocate 75 megahertz of radio spectrum to mobile services. Their definition of mobile services was virtually everything. Air to ground, radio/telephone (which ultimately became cellular) and dispatch services – two way radio. It was AT&T's assertion that they could do all of these things much more efficiently than competitive industry. AT&T was of course at that time THE phone company and thought they were the only ones capable of doing that. We at Motorola objected to that thesis and suggested that a competitive business was more appropriate – that mixing these services would in fact make the use of the spectrum very inefficient. There ensued a huge regulatory and political battle. The bottom line is that these three services were in fact, allocated separate frequency bands and each of the resultant services operated competitively. The most significant change (relative to today's cellular industry and the future of telephony) was that AT&T's proposal for cellular telephone was a car telephones service. I vigorously objected to that viewpoint. Our view was that the portable telephone was the way to go and that view, of course, stimulated the development of this first portable cellular telephone. Motorola wanted to make a dramatic demonstration to the FCC and to the legislators in Congress that this was the way of the future. What better way to do that than to build a system and have it working? We demonstrated that working system first for the FCC and for the Congress in Washington and then we did a public demonstration in New York. We built a real cellular system in New York so that a user could walk down that city's streets while talking on a phone. That sounds mundane today but you cannot imagine the otherwise sophisticated New Yorkers gaping at us.

Between the introduction of the cellar portable, in 1973, and ArrayComm, there's a huge gap. In the interim I moved into the corporate staff and ran all of Motorola's research and development for some years, as Vice President of R&D. I then left Motorola to form, with two partners, a new company called Cellular Business Systems, Inc. This company did the billing and management systems for most of the cellular operators in the beginning years of cellular. That company was sold to Cincinnati Bell in 1986. Many of the products that we developed at that time survived with a company called Convergys, which is now a multi billion dollar billing company. After that, my wife and I started a couple of other companies, but basically, I was in semi-retirement until 1992 when a mathematician approached me from Stanford. He had this wonderful idea of how to create very intelligent antenna systems that had the potential of virtually revolutionizing the wireless industry. I had, at that time, people calling me every week or two with one idea or another, some of which were very good, but not many of which were extremely interesting to me. This guy insisted that he had to tell me about this and the only time we could find to meet was at a conference. I told him the only time I had available was in the morning, but that I usually went running in the morning. He insisted that he go running with me. There we were running on the waterfront of New Orleans with me gasping for air and this guy cruising along explaining this technology to me. It turns out that Dr. Richard Roy was a real athlete. The first encounter evolved into several other less athletic meetings. I agreed to advise the company on the order of a day or two a month, and I've been working seven days a week ever since early in 1992. So that's the genesis of ArrayComm. The perspective that Dick Roy brought to this was very different than what people had previously perceived as being smart antennas. We engineers think of groups of antennas in the sense of the way phased array antennas were used as far back as World War II. These antenna systems literally created radio beams for radar systems. Dick Roy was a mathematician not an engineer and he looked upon these antenna systems as solving a mathematical problem. You have a bunch of sensors (the antennas) and each sensor has a different signal. You're trying to receive one of many signals out in the world and you're trying to reject a bunch of other ones. He stated all of this as a mathematical problem and concluded that if he could solve that problem fast enough, than he could improve the nature of communications by orders of magnitude. At the time that we started the company, there were no processors available that could do this fast enough. It would have taken something on the order of a Cray Computer to do that. We were forced to demonstrate our technology using simulations. Today we are solving these problems in some 50,000 base stations all around the world. The kind of processing I'm talking about, that was in a Cray computer in 1992 is now available in a chip set that we buy from Motorola or Texas Instruments for $115. There have been some huge changes. The thing that made a smart antennae, we call it an adaptive array processing system, is convergence of the ability to do large amounts of processing at low cost and the need of the wireless industry to have that capability.

Enjoying Work

Today I'm enjoying most the intellectual challenge and the understanding that we really are having an impact on the wireless world. If there is one characteristic of ArrayComm that people notice when they come and visit us, it's that we are a collection of very smart and very dedicated people. The average age of the people in the company is less than half my age. Keeping up with these guys keeps me young. However, more significantly, ArrayComm is performing a really important task. People describe the success of the wireless industry in terms of the billion of subscribers that will be using cellular phones in the next year or two. That's misleading! In fact, there is still a long way to go. The penetration of actual minutes of talking time is still quite small, for obvious reasons. Cellular doesn't work as well as wired phones and it costs too much. There's no reason why a wireless system can't be every bit as good as a wired system and yet we all know what the perception of cellular is. If there's one common experience, it's the dropped call, and I know it has happened to most of us. You're in the middle of a telephone call and suddenly there's nobody there. This poor performance is not fundamental to wireless. It's the result of overloading the wireless system. Either carriers have to be satisfied with fewer people on a channel, which means they make less money, or there has to be technology that works better. The fact that we are creating just that kind of technology is a great source of satisfaction to those of us at ArrayComm.

Wireless' Development

The principles that we proved back in 1973 are being tested once again. The fundamental principle was the importance of mobility and portability for personal communications. People now use cellular phones as second nature and would have a great deal of difficulty getting along without them. The same thing will be true with the Internet. There's a huge potential for the Internet to bring services, content, and all kinds of devices that will make people's lives easier, more comfortable and more productive. Certainly, you are not going to avail yourselves all those things if you have to plug into a wall to get them, so we're working very hard at creating the same kind of freedom from wires that cellular offered, but for the Internet. The real value of the Internet will happen when there is an always-on capability that is ubiquitous, that you can get in a portable sense, that you can get wherever you are, and at high speed (high speed meaning a megabit per second). More importantly, the wireless industry has to grow out of its monopoly heritage. The legacy of the whole communications industry goes back to the beginning, where one telephone company provided all the communications services. That is a legacy that exists in virtually every country in the world. In the U.S. it was AT&T. In Britain, BT, in Japan, NTT. The nature of the monopoly business is that the carrier runs the business, the carrier owns the customer, the carrier does all the marketing and decides what the products are. That's not how real consumer businesses grow and prosper. And yet, competition is what makes the consumer industry thrive because it turns out consumers are very complex. There are many, many markets and very clever people attacking different segments of the market that makes a lot of different segments successful. Phone companies just don't operate that way.

Look at what's happened with cellular, for example. Theoretically there's competition in cellular and yet the services offered by the different companies are identical. The only thing that they battle on is the pricing plan and their focus is on the high usage subscriber – the rest of the constituencies be damned! There are many constituencies that have a need for wireless communications and that can afford to pay for it. This neglect has to change in the future and it will. There's no way that seven carriers in a city are all going to offer the same service and all be viable. The fundamentals of business dictate that the leader in a business will be most profitable and most successful, and that the number two can be successful. Number three's going to struggle and anybody beyond that better go find some other business to be in. What we're going to see in the telecommunications industry is a move toward open markets and open architecture of systems, competitive systems. There'll be a lot of people focusing on different segments of the market.

Unfinished Business

I'm very disappointed with the performance of cellular today, just in the way that I described earlier in this chapter. The carriers have to get the performance of their systems so that the performance is comparable to wire line. There's no reason why that shouldn't be true. The manifestation of poor performance is the fact that, not withstanding there is a subscriber penetration rate that's approaching 20% of the population of the U.S. (and it's higher in other countries), there's still a lot of room for growth in cellular subscriber penetration – not the correct measure. The real measure is what proportion of the minutes of talking you do is done on wireless compared to wire line. Believe it or not that's still less than 5% in the U.S. So if there is a message there, it's that there is a lot of improvement that has to be done for just voice communications. I have every confidence that some carrier will start to differentiate himself by offering a higher quality of service and that people will in fact pay for that.

The Effect of 3G

3G will provide an incremental improvement in voice services. It has a slightly higher capacity and therefore has the potential of getting either better quality or lower cost.

3G also offers incremental improvement in the data capability, but not very much. The order of 64 kilobit per second service will be available. Insofar as you can offer a voice service with an ancillary 64 or so kbs data service there are going to be some new capabilities with 3G. But 3G is only incrementally better than the 2G systems. What I believe is going to happen in the future is that there are going to be many different kinds of systems. There is pressure to create a worldwide standard. That won't happen. The wonderful thing about standards is that there are so many of them. There will be different standards all optimized for different kinds of markets. 3G is a voice centric system. There are going to be data centric systems and Internet centric systems and we're going to see a lot of different constituencies served.

Broadband Wireless

There are things that wireless does that are better than wire line and the opposite is true as well. The priority for wireless is for the things that you can only do wirelessly – that is mobility and portability. I see those features as being the really important things of the future. The issue of broadband fixed service is just one of competition between fiber and DSL and LMDS and infra-red and MMDS. There's a role for all of them. Each offers advantages under certain conditions. I find those fixed services much less interesting than broadband delivery to people that are mobile. In every other case it's only a question of whether it's easier to get a cable wired into your house or building or to deliver it over the air. Having said all that, they're all going to be huge industries. The need for bandwidth is going to keep increasing over the years and technology is going to be hard pressed, although successful, in keeping up with that need. We're going to use every means to do that and that includes fiber, wire, and a bunch of different wireless capabilities.

Mainstreaming Wireless

The optimizing of a system to do one thing, and that is do deliver high-speed data to people that are portable, but not necessarily moving with an always-on capability, is going to engender a huge number of applications. I'm talking about things like cameras that deliver their pictures to a website virtually instantly, or if you're a journalist, to your editor instantly. I'm talking about downloading music, about games that can be played wherever the user is, about public safety, having police officers being able to access huge databases at the scene of a crime, about tele-medicine, the ability to either treat people or have people treat themselves when they're sick instead of having to go to the hospital by transmitting diagnostic information through the Internet. All of those things, and many that I can't think of, are going to be available when there is a true high speed Internet capability that is portable and wireless.

The Importance of Capital

If you want to talk about wireless in general the kinds of numbers that it's taken to build the systems and the hardware we're talking about have been huge and venture capital has not performed an extraordinary role. I think that's changing to a large extent although ArrayComm itself was funded primarily by institutions and through strategic investment. But the industry is changing. It's changing just because of the comments I made earlier about moving away from the monopoly legacy to a bunch of competitive businesses that are focused on niche markets. These are huge niches, so now we have the opportunity of relatively small companies attacking specific issues or addressing specific markets or specific areas of technology. Today there are five telecommunications companies that pretty much command the wireless world. You know who they are. It starts with Ericsson, Lucent, Motorola, Northern Telecom, Nokia and after that you go way down. I think you're going to see smaller companies with unique technical capabilities that will be chipping away at the market and focusing in on very specific things. When you do that the venture capitalists start making a contribution. One example is AirNet, who built a software base station for GSM. That company is starting to make fairly important headway and they're funded by venture capitalists. Some of our competitors in the smart antenna business are venture capital funded so I think that they're impact is starting to increase. However, in wireless it is not really as significant as it has been with the Internet businesses.

Markets' Effect on Wireless

The wireless industry is a very complex industry. Maybe that's my perception because I've lived wireless my whole career. That's all I've ever really done from my first job when I started at Motorola in 1954, and I've been working in wireless ever since. So maybe I have a very narrow perception. The public markets tend to take a very superficial view of things, so when they decided that paging was not going to be important, the valuations of the paging industry virtually collapsed. The fact is that paging is going to be around for a long time and paging operators have the potential of providing very useful services and doing very important things. The same thing is happening today with cellular and the public markets have decided that the carriers have spent too much money on spectrum and that the build out is going to be much slower, especially of 3G, and that is true. The financial markets have lost sight of the fact that the industry is still in it's infancy, that this growth is really what the public market should be concerned about, is going to continue for many, many years. I find that the viewpoints of the public market tend to make it very difficult for the industry and the carriers. Having said that, I don't know if there's any better way to fund the growth of the industry, there is just no alternative.

Government Regulation

Licensing is a very complex problem mostly because I think there are going to be a bunch of 3G capabilities. This initiative occurred in Japan and Europe and is kind of an outgrowth of the GSM concept. GSM has enormous advantage in the sense that it is ubiquitous. You can go practically anywhere in the world and use a GSM phone, but on the other hand it is a standard and standards can be restrictive. The fact is that the future that I see, is one with lots of different standards and different kinds of systems to solve different kinds of problems. I don't think there is going to be just one system. The issue is not so much generating spectrum for 3G, but generating spectrum for all of the different applications. The fact is that there are tons of spectrum available. The real problem with spectrum allocation is not 3G or any one system, but how efficiently the spectrum is used. The best example of how not to do that is what's going on in the television broadcast industry. We're operating today in the broadcast industry under technical rules that were written, would you believe, in the 1940's. And yet television technology has advanced by many orders of magnitude. It's going to take another ten years to get digital TV in place, which will use the spectrum a great deal better. Meanwhile we're wasting hundreds of megahertz of radio spectrum that could be used for other functions.

I created a concept that I call Cooper's law, kind of tongue in cheek, but it's really true. I did an analysis of how effectively people could use the radio spectrum for personal communications. It's very simple. How many conversations can you hold in a given amount of spectrum over a given amount of area? It all started 105 years ago when Marconi made his first transmission, which was point-to-point using a spark transmitter. At that time you could conduct one conversation in the whole world in the whole spectrum. It turns out that we have essentially doubled the capability of using the spectrum every 30 months, every 2½ years, for the last 105 years and if you work out those numbers it turns out that we use the spectrum a trillion times more effectively than Marconi did. The really exciting part of this is that we now know that this could go on for another 60 years with technology that we know about. Never mind new inventions that will happen. Here we are with the spectrum getting more valuable every 2½ years and yet the nature of the way spectrum is allocated is once somebody gets a hold of a lump of spectrum they develop a power base and they hold on to it for dear life. The real challenge is for the FCC and all the regulatory bodies. How do they get the legacy users of spectrum to release their hold and make room for the new technologies and the new ways to use spectrum more efficiently?

The interesting thing about radio spectrum is that there has never really been a shortage of spectrum. Whatever shortages there are, whatever excessive prices people are paying are artificially created. They're created because of the manner in which spectrum is allocated. Look what's happened with the spectrum that was auctioned off for PCS. The FCC made some efforts to try to get small businesses involved and get a variety of applications, but the bottom line is that for some reason or another most of the spectrum, especially the most valuable part, has gotten into the hands of the same people that are providing original cellular services. A number of the people that have tried to do innovative things have essentially gone bankrupt because of the effects of the way the spectrum was allocated and how the public markets have perceived the wireless industry. It's a very complicated issue only because in the short term the spectrum is not very valuable if you think about it. We can only do so many things. The markets are only so big and the people that are spending these huge billions of dollars in spectrum in Europe, for example, are going to be hard pressed to make those expenditures pay off. In the long term Cooper's law is right, that spectrum is going to be extraordinarily valuable. The real challenge is going to be to hang on to the spectrum and stay in business long enough until technology and the ability to mine all of these interesting markets catch up to what people paid for the spectrum.

Worldwide Wireless

I really believe that in the U.S. we are going to start seeing new players. People are already talking about an auction for some 700 MHz spectrums and about how some of the buyers of that are going to be non-traditional. They're going to be people like Microsoft and AOL and perhaps Cisco. So we are seeing a trend with new players and hopefully lots of new competition. I like to think that maybe we'll see some ventures. These are real gorillas that are going after this spectrum, but meanwhile it is competitive. I think the same thing is going to happen in Europe and Japan, but at a much slower rate because the telephone companies, the monopolies, are much more deeply entrenched in those countries. Each country is a little different. Notwithstanding the EEC there is a lot of competition going on in Britain, less in other countries, but I think we're going to be seeing a lot more true competition. Ultimately every country is going to be in a similar situation as the U.S. Telecommunications will be truly competitive and will have lots of entities in the markets.

I don't think the U.S. is at a disadvantage to Europe and Asia. And that's not just sheer patriotism. I think that competition may appear to be inefficient just as democracy appears to be inefficient compared to dictatorship, but ultimately free markets end up with the right answer whereas dictatorships and monopolies do not. They operate more efficiently, but they don't avail themselves of the new technologies. They don't avail themselves the ability to go after market niches and changing markets. I think the U.S. has the advantage in that respect and that we're going to be generating lots of technology, but also lots of different businesses and market applications ahead of other people. The thing that would appear to contradict that statement is the fact that Japan, NTT is the leader in 3G at the moment and they are starting to grasp the concept of open platform.

i-Mode is one particularly interesting area. This is a data application that is laid on top of a voice centric system, like third-generation or second-generation today, that lets outsiders create applications for the telephone company system. Unfortunately, what NTT is doing is at such a low data rate that the applications are almost laughable. They're still making money and they're giving us a little picture into the future. What's going to happen is that the U.S. is going to implement these things in a much more meaningful way and once again we're going to leapfrog the Japanese.

The whole concept of cellular was created in the U.S. Bell Laboratories invented cellular and Motorola and my team modified the concept dramatically, but the Japanese thought that they were going to leapfrog us and built their own cellular system and were on the air before the U.S. It turns out that their system was not at all successful and it took the Japanese ten years to catch up to the U.S. I suspect the same thing is going to happen with the 3G efforts. The Japanese are the first out there with 3G systems, but when it comes to the real applications and the execution, you're going to see some very exciting things happen in the U.S.

One of the things ArrayComm did was based upon the knowledge that most of the people of the world have never talked on any kind of a telephone and that there are waiting lists in many countries of literally millions that can afford to have telephones that don't. We invented a wireless local loop system that has the capability of bringing telephone, fax and data up to a 128kb to people in third world countries or any country for that matter at costs lower than wired systems. It turns out that we've had a lot of trouble selling those systems, or our licensees have had trouble selling them. It turns out that countries tend to serve the constituencies with the most money so they're spending lots of money in third world countries on building out cellular systems that serve the elite, but they're not spending a lot of money reaching the populace. Ultimately that's going to change. It's been demonstrated repeatedly that there is a direct correlation between the ability to bring communications to people and the productivity of a country. If the third world countries are going to break out, or if they're going to emerge, than they have to develop a telecommunications capability for people much more effectively than they have.

I guess the best example of an underdeveloped country that's managed to do this is China. The most advanced wireless data system in the world today is PHS. PHS is the Personal Handyphone Service. The concept was developed in the States, interestingly enough, and was picked up and improved by the Japanese. The PHS system in Japan is the most advanced wireless data system in the world. There are all kinds of interesting devices operating at speeds today at 64kb going up to 128kb per second and perhaps even faster and at very low cost. There are PC cards that you can plug into a notebook to allow the computer to be used wirelessly ubiquitously. There are cameras where you can talk to somebody and see their face, there are notepads that you can write in Chinese characters and have people get the message immediately, these are all products that are in use daily today by millions of people. In China today in the smaller cities, smaller cities being defined as city on the order of a million, millions of people are now availing themselves of PHS service. People use the PHS phone as their primary telephone because it costs the same or less than a landline. These people have the capability of a whole bunch of things that wired telephones don't have, but at lower cost and very often in places where you don't even have wired service.

Advice for Startups

The advice you give to any startup is to raise enough money to achieve your worst-case plan – and then get more. You can never have too much. The greatest sin that a startup can encounter is running out of cash – and almost all of them do. The challenge is to develop a story that is persuasive enough that you can attract the right kind of partners and make sure that your partners always keep your venture funded adequately. People at startup companies have to be optimistic. If they are too optimistic, their revenues never come as quickly as they expect, so they run out of money and either go out of business or they get taken advantage of by the financial community – that's called "restructuring." The people that put their sweat into the businesses are not the ones who end up succeeding. So startups require a balance of optimism and realism. Without the optimism you can't attract capital. There also has to be an element of realism that ensures that you don't run out of money.

On Leadership

Real leadership is getting people to do things they would not otherwise do and having them enjoy doing that. When you're dealing with smart people, they can't be fooled. They'll follow when they believe and when they respect the leader.

A leader has to truly understand his or her business. If one is going to have impact on that business, the only way to really understand it is to live it. By living it one cannot be theoretical. If you're in the wireless business, you have to be a wireless user and you have to experiment and truly understand the essence of who it is that uses the technology. You have to understand the basis of the technology and how the technology will advance. The significance of what I'm saying is if you look at Silicon Valley today you'll observe the phenomenon of the get-rich-quick phenomenon. People feel that if they don't start a business and do an IPO in a year and walk away with hundreds of millions of dollars, they're failures. How can you truly understand a business or a market unless you have first gone through and started a business and finished it and understood what the process is and then truly understand the nature of what you're doing and then do something significant. A number of things can happen in a matter of a year or so. Notwithstanding everything people say about how everything is accelerating at our age, it still takes a couple of years to develop a product. It takes a couple of years to really create a market presence so you can't really do anything materially significant in less than four or five years. If you start out with the attitude that you're really going to understand things and that it's going to take that long, you do have the opportunity of doing something important. If you start out assuming that you're going to make a quick buck and bail out, you'll never have a really significant impact because you can't do anything important in a short period of time.

A pioneer in the wireless communications industry, Martin invented and introduced the first portable cellular phone in 1973. During 29 years with Motorola, he built and ran both its paging and cellular businesses and served as Corporate Director of Research and Development. Products introduced by Martin have had cumulative sales volume of over $50 billion. Upon leaving Motorola, Martin co-founded Cellular Business Systems Inc. and led it to dominate the cellular billing industry with a 75% market share before selling it to Cincinnati Bell. Martin has been granted six patents in the communications field and has been widely published on various aspects of communications technology and on management of research and development. He has recently been inducted into the RCR Wireless Hall of Fame and Red Herring magazine has chosen Martin as one of the Top 10

Entrepreneurs of 2000. He holds a B.S. and an M.S. in Electrical Engineering from Illinois Institute of Technology.

ROBERT GEMMELL
Bringing Wireless Into the Mainstream
Digital Wireless
CEO

Attention to Wireless

I think people are recognizing the positive effect that wireless technology can have on the way things are being done. People are seeing the impact that the cellular business has had on productivity, on their ability to communicate and stay in touch. I'm old enough to remember not having cell phones. At a Christmas party in 1982, I heard a guy talking about putting some money into a cellular startup company, and he really thought that was going to make him a lot of money. People were kind of intrigued by that because it was a fairly new thing and was considered a very high-risk investment at that time. Cellular technology was not an obvious big win when it was first happening, and for a number of years that was a pretty risky business. Some of the service providers didn't make it. When you look back and see how it's turned out, it's hard to imagine. It has been an incredibly successful business, and the companies that have hung in there and done well have done extremely well. Just think what the impact of that has been in terms of connectivity and productivity. It seems funny now that business people used to actually routinely pull off the road and go to a pay phone just to stay in touch with the office and to make things happen.

One thing that I have seen with every segment of the wireless industry is that everything good that you can imagine happening does happen, although it happens a little slower than you think it might. Starting in the early '90s, there were a lot of projections about wireless data and wireless local area networking. If you look at market research reports from that time, a lot of what was talked about is starting to happen, but it's starting a few years later than expected. I think people want to translate what's happened with cellular voice to that kind of mobility, flexibility, and productivity with data. They're seeing how those improvements can apply to data, in terms of not just connectivity and voice but connectivity with computing devices and sensing devices. I think it's getting a lot of attention because people are starting to see these new applications, and they're imagining the impact that they can make. They're seeing a huge business opportunity.

The Benefits of Wireless

Consumers and companies will benefit most from these new technologies. These technologies enable huge increases in company productivity when they're applied in the work place, and they have a huge benefit to individuals and consumers. Communications and connectivity are valuable to businesses for productivity. They're valuable to individuals for personal reasons, to stay in touch with people conveniently. And of course, investors stand to benefit from the value these technologies offer to customers.

From our perspective, the new WaveBolt family of wireless Internet access products that we are introducing will greatly benefit Internet users and ISPs (Internet Service Providers) worldwide. Internet users in the U.S. want higher speed access and potential Internet users around the world just want to get connected. Less than 6% of the U.S. residential population has high-speed access, and with current deployment and technology options, more than 70% have no way of getting it in the foreseeable future from DSL or cable. Now add to that an estimated 250 million PCs that will be shipped internationally over the next five years into regions with limited wired telephone infrastructures and you have a huge number of people who want access and can't get it.

As Internet users actively seek faster connections and in many countries simply connection, ISPs need cost effective and easily deployable alternatives to meet this demand. For a rapid return on investment, ISPs want to spend less than $400 per subscriber, which must cover subscriber equipment, access point equipment, and installation costs.

Wireless' Development

I think the most exciting thing is something we're involved in. As I stated earlier, we're going to bring the next wave of Internet users online with wireless Internet access, and I think that's terribly exciting. The Internet is still in its early stages; I know that's hard to believe because the Internet seems so pervasive to us, but it is nothing compared to what it's going to be. The Internet is going to have many times more users coming online over the next few years.

The Wireless Industry

Current Internet usage is about 150 million users worldwide, with 62 million in the U.S., but those are small numbers compared to what's going to happen. There's another wave of Internet users that is going to come online around the world, and new users are going to be coming online with much higher bandwidth capacity available to them. I think the most exciting part is that the number of people on the Internet is going to go up dramatically as wireless connectivity is made available to the mass market. The other exciting trend will be the higher speed services that are going to be offered and the new applications coming online that will leverage those higher speeds.

None of this would happen without wireless, because you simply cannot deploy wired infrastructure fast enough and you can't make a business case for doing it. It's too difficult and expensive, and it cannot happen fast enough. The model for this is to look at how voice has expanded internationally through cellular networks. If you go to regions around the world, Latin America or Asia for example, everybody has cell phones. That is the telephone system. The telephone network internationally is largely a cellular network because that was the way to deploy a telephone network. It wasn't to go lay copper and fiber because you couldn't do that fast enough. It was too expensive, too difficult, and so it didn't develop that way. The telephone network has expanded and developed internationally through cellular, and data and Internet access is also going to expand wirelessly because that's the only way you can do it.

In the United States, subscribers are wired but want faster data connections than those offered by traditional dial-up services. Despite all the hype, this demand is still unmet by cable modem and digital subscriber line (DSL) connections. The limitations of DSL and cable technology for last-mile Internet access to regions with low population densities are huge.

The Importance of Capital

Funding sources like venture capitalists are critical to wireless. It takes a lot of R&D, it takes a lot of investment and scaling and manufacturing and developing sales channels, but it takes a lot of capital to fund product development. That's really what's happening right now. You've got a lot of companies that are developing products that are really going to change the way things are done with network access. That initial funding, until companies develop to a point where they can get into public markets, comes from the venture capital market.

The Effects of the Markets on Wireless

The second stage or so of development for the companies is the expansion capital source. The first stage is venture capital and then expansion capital comes from public markets, so the next stage is equally critical.

I have always taken it as a given that even technology companies are meant to have earnings. I think that the public markets are pretty rational in demanding the earnings, at least for companies that reach a certain scale. If a company goes public and its revenues are at still a fairly modest level but the company is growing rapidly, then I think the public markets still accept some losses at that stage. They look at the companies' revenues, and assess the impact that scaling up will have to determine the company's prospects for achieving profitability. They look at whether the company is growing very rapidly and whether they believe that the company's going to achieve that scale. And if that's the case, then I think the market is still accepting relatively short-term losses. But I think once a company reaches a certain size the market is pretty rational in terms of expecting earnings. I think that's pretty much as it should be. I don't view that as a problem.

Worldwide Wireless

I think the international opportunity is absolutely enormous. Many regions of the world have very poor telephony-wired infrastructure, and they have developed their telephone networks via cellular. Now there's this huge demand for data – specifically Internet access – and there's going to be a lot of packet voice traffic on that network.

Let me talk about the major regions and then think about how I might rank them. The major regions are Latin America, Eastern Europe, Asia and then probably also North Africa, and the Middle East. Those are some of the booming areas. It's a little difficult to rank those, but I would probably rank Asia as having some of the most exciting opportunities. I think Latin America is also a very interesting region. You've got a population base that has a growing sector that is demanding and can afford to pay for higher-speed Internet access or just Internet access at all. In these markets you've got something that looks more like the U.S. about five years ago. You've got ISPs starting up in these regions at a similar stage of development as some of the major ISPs in the U.S. about five years ago. What I mean by interesting in Asia and Latin America is the numbers of people there who can afford to pay for Internet access and are demanding it.

I really don't think the U.S. based companies are at a disadvantage to Europe or Asia. I think the world markets expect a lot of this technology to come from the U.S., and I don't sense significant protectionism in place to block products coming from U.S. companies.

Key Industry Players

The wireless business is still a new and evolving market and it is very difficult to predict who will ultimately be the key players.

But as for what it takes to make this happen with carriers in the U.S., there really are two main issues, what we call barriers to deployment for these types of networks. One is the ease of technical installation, especially of the customer premise's equipment (CPE), and the second is the equipment price.

From an ease of installation standpoint, ISPs ideally would like for the end user subscribers to be able to install their own equipment without having major technical glitches that require a professional installer to actually come on site and do technical support, especially on an ongoing basis.

It's bad enough to have to use a professional installer at all, but having recurring problems is something that none of the service providers are well prepared to deal with in terms of having the resources or a business model to do that and still make money.

The other issue is the price or cost of the equipment, which must cover subscriber equipment, access point equipment, and installation costs. Based on our research with ISPs, we developed a marketing model that we have that I think illustrates our perception of what makes this market happen from a pricing standpoint. In our opinion, there is market pricing in place for what people will or can pay for higher-speed Internet access in the United States. Look at the cost of getting high-speed Internet access through either DSL or cable modem in areas where it's available and there's penetration of the market with those technologies. In general people pay $40 to $50 per month to get Internet service through some kind of DSL or cable modem-type connection. Dial-up Internet typically is still $15 to $20 per month, so what you're looking at there is market pricing of about $20 to $40 per month for mass market acceptance of Internet connectivity.

The other part of the pricing equation is the kind of return on investment or payback period service providers need to get when they deploy this type of equipment. The answer is one year. It's a pretty easy business case for them to deploy the network with a one-year payback, especially on the subscriber end of the equipment. You start stretching that to two or three years, and given the inevitable life cycle of new products and new technologies, you can imagine this gets pretty scary. I think at three years you don't have a business, at two years you have a painful business, at a year you've got a business case that the service providers feel good about because they will see a rapid return on investment. What all of this means is that for a one-year return on investment the equipment and deployment cost must be $350 to $400 per subscriber for it to make sense both from a market pricing standpoint and a payback standpoint to the service providers.

We really believe in that model, and we kind of backed into it by talking to service providers for a long time about their perception about where cost needed to be for the customer premises equipment to make sense to them. We were consistently hearing $350 to $400 per subscriber where it would start to make sense for them to do it on a large-scale basis. You can go out with more expensive equipment and sell it for businesses to get very high-speed access, but to get it into the mainstream, we really believe that this $350 to $400 per subscriber is the beginning, and I think it needs to even go lower than that. But that's the beginning of where you can start making an impact on the market. The bottom line is that the equipment being introduced to the marketplace right now is on average at least double that. If you talk to equipment manufacturers privately, they're going to admit that at least for the next two or three years they're only going after the very tip of the pyramid, primarily business users because they're deploying equipment that cannot achieve the price point or ease of installation requirements for a mass-market deployment.

Bringing Wireless Into the Mainstream

The Wireless Industry

In terms of when mobile Internet access is going to become more mainstream, there's some real technical challenges to doing that that involve dealing with fairly typical fading conditions inherent in radio networks. Typical problems include multi-path fading or may simply be getting interruptions in the link, where things are in the way between you and the cell tower. The important thing is that whenever you hear any kind of problem when you're having a voice conversation on your cell phone, from a data standpoint you have a non-functional link. Voice is so much easier than data, and I don't know if people really know that. Data must have a higher-quality radio link and do some rather sophisticated kinds of equalization and error coding to achieve a mobile data network that deals with all kinds fading and with things and buildings getting in the way. So there's a reason it hasn't been successfully deployed yet, but it is going to happen and I think that a lot of the work being done on third-generation cellular is working to achieve that.

With 3G, you're probably going to initially have a network that at least deals with bursts of data very well. It is unlikely that 3G is going to deal with continuous data; it's not really even designed to do that. You'll hear specifications for data rates for third-generation cellular networks like 144kb per second. If you really look at it carefully, what they're talking about is burst data rates. Nobody's going to guarantee continuous data rates at speeds like that because it's very, very difficult to do. So in the first wave of 3G deployments, you're going to have something much faster than what you can do over the cellular network now, which is really slow. You can go out and get a modem that runs on the cell phone right now, but you're going to get hardly any through put. 3G is going to be a lot better than that, but it's not going to be like sitting there on DSL. You're going to get it in bursts, so it's going to work well for email, it's going to be tolerable or adequate for some web surfing, but it's not going to be like having 144k fixed point or wireline connection, where it's going to be a lot of fun to play games or look at video or stuff like that. 3G is going to take a good while to deploy. I don't mean to sound pessimistic, but my perception is that Japan is leading the way as the first country to deploy 3G. Europe was supposed to be second, but I'm reading things about 3G really slowing down in Europe, that the capital expenditures to do it are starting to be overwhelming. U.S. is then behind Europe. I don't know when we're going to have 3G in the U.S., but it's many years away and I'm not qualified to predict exactly. I have an opinion that we're at least five to seven years away from 3G in the U.S.

I think anything is possible. I think they'll be continuous improvements and additions to the network, but it is an ultimate challenge. Maybe there'll be some completely different technology that's developed that makes that easier to do. I doubt that it's going to be done using something that looks a lot like the current cellular network. I think that they'll be some different approach. There's a point where saturating enough access points is one way to deal with it, but there are physical limitations on how much you can do that. There's already tremendous resistance to adding cell towers in residential areas. The ultimate thing to achieve a real good radio link is a clear line of sight and providing that to mobile users is impossible. As long as you don't have line of sight, it means that you're getting signals inherently through reflected paths, and as long as you're doing that, you're going to have fades, so it's not an easy problem.

The Cost of Building the Wireless Infrastructure

If you go out with an expensive network, you're only going to sell it to the upper tier, large enterprise segment of the market. Going out with expensive equipment means that you're not doing a mass-market deployment. We took this into consideration when we developed our product for the residential and small business market. That is why we are offering equipment to ISPs that will allow a rapid return on investment.

I think that carriers are making decisions right now about what they're going to do, about the equipment they're going to deploy. They are at the point right now of doing trials and pilot deployments, and I think that this is the year for trials and making decisions. I think you're going to start to see the large deployments starting around the third or fourth quarter in 2001. I think the business will hit full stride starting in 2002-2003. In terms of when they're going to be finished, I don't know if you're ever finished, but I think it's going to start to become commonplace especially in 2002.

Issues around 3G

I don't think licensing fees are the issue as much as I think there are plenty of technical issues. There are a number of competing standards, I don't think you could even say for sure what the network's going to be. Even in Europe where the path is clear, they're going to go to a 3G version of GSM. It's still taking a long time to do it, so you can imagine in the U.S. where you have TDMA, CDMA, and GSM getting into the fray, it's going to take longer just to sort all that out. The products aren't ready. The technology's not quite ready, and the path in terms of what technology approach is even going to be used isn't clear. Those are the reasons I can say with some confidence that 3G is going to happen slower in the U.S. than people think. I don't mean to be pessimistic, but that's just the way it is. Frankly, that's the way the cell phone network was too.

Government Regulation

For the unlicensed segment of the business that we're playing in right now, I think the regulations are mature. There is a worldwide regulation for operating unlicensed in the band that we're focused on most heavily right now, which is the 2.4 GHz band, and that's one of the things that's really letting us move quickly and giving us confidence in terms of working with service providers on large-scale deployments. Those regulatory developments that impacted what we're doing now happened three or four years ago, so what we've got is harmonization of FCC rules with rules around the world. There was compatibility between the European rules and the FCC rules for the 2.4 GHz band, and we've seen every country around the world fall in line with those rules. Our products have been CE marked and in the process of doing so, have certifications in all the European Union countries. We're seeing this now in every country around the world, so the good news for us is that we're past that stage of risk. I can't speak for some of the other segments; I'm not sure what role the FCC is going to play in the 3G standards for example.

Advice to Startups

I would just suggest that they be aware of developing unique products and keeping customer and market needs in mind. I've seen cases where if you get too far away from the customer, it's just too easy to develop interesting technology. A common thing is to develop interesting technology that misses out on the market pricing element. It'd be nice in a technology business to believe that developing technology will create a market, but the truth is that the beginning and the end really is the market need and delivering the right product at the right price, and they just can't forget that. It's more than just technology. You need to know what need you're filling and understand what the market can bear in terms of price.

A second piece of advice would be to be prepared to move quickly, get products to market quickly, but also be prepared to have some patience. A lot of different segments of the wireless market have taken some time to develop, and keeping that history in mind means that you have some patience and some staying power.

On Leadership

I think starting out with a good technical background was important. I knew that I didn't want to be an engineer forever, but it was helpful getting that exposure because if you want to be a visionary about conceiving new products and creating new markets, at least understanding what's possible is really helpful. Being able to understand what's realistic and what the engineering team can do realistically and the time frame they can do it in has been really helpful as well.

Another thing is I think the importance of being involved in sales is underestimated. I have an MBA and that's nice, but getting an MBA and then just getting into sort of strategy and marketing isn't the same as actually getting out on the street and actually talking to customers. I think it's important to never really lose your connection to the customer base. Really talk to them about what they need and what they're trying to do and what you can do to help them. I think that is really kind of the beginning and the end of businesses. You've got to deliver products that meet customer expectations and what people need, which sounds so incredibly obvious, but try not to get yourself in a vacuum just doing exotic technology. There's got to be a hands-on understanding of what customers want.

Also, avoid becoming too much of a specialist in any one thing. That's not easy in this industry. When you get into this industry, especially as an engineer, it's pretty easy to get locked into doing one area of technology. If that's what you want to do, if you want to be a specialist in RF design or software, that is a tremendous career path. But it kind of works against you if you want to become a general manager or a president of a company. You need broader experience, and you've got to work to keep your career from getting locked into too much specialization.

The Wireless Industry

Robert Gemmell has provided innovative leadership to Digital Wireless Corporation (DWC) as CEO and chairman of the board since 1995. He successfully positioned DWC as a major supplier of wireless spread-spectrum (a technology he developed) products for diverse industrial markets, and continues to do so for industrial and last-mile Internet-access markets. Mr. Gemmell initially joined DWC in 1992 as vice president of marketing and sales, where he succeeded in restoring the company to stable and profitable growth without raising outside capital. He also led the company into various successful OEM-partner channels and international markets.

Prior to joining DWC, Mr. Gemmell was a marketing and technology-transfer consultant to Georgia Tech and approximately 100 startup companies in Atlanta. Previously, he worked six years in marketing management roles for General Electric and Intel Corporation. Mr. Gemmell first developed spread spectrum radio technology while at the National Security Agency from 1975 through 1979. Additionally, he holds two patents for CMOS analog integrated circuits for telecom applications, which he designed during 1980-1982. Mr. Gemmell's career in electronics and technology spans more than 25 years.

Mr. Gemmell received bachelor's and master's degrees in electrical engineering from Georgia Tech, graduating with highest honors. He also completed the executive MBA program at Duke University in 1985. Additionally, he is a member of Georgia Tech's Academy of Distinguished Engineering Alumni.

ALEX LAATS
VoiceXML
Informio
CEO and Co-Founder

Background Information

I started off in the technology world at MIT as an undergrad, and I received degrees in physics and math. But I had a very strong itch to get into the business side of the world. This was in the late '80s, and I made a decision to go to law school, a rather indirect route but nevertheless a route into the business side, and I got into Harvard Law School. I graduated from law school and surprised myself by actually practicing law at a firm in Boston that represents high-tech corporate clients in software and other computer systems areas as well as investment bankers, underwriters, and the like. That was an excellent experience, but it even increased my entrepreneurial itch to get into the business side. In 1994 I left the law firm to go to MIT to work in the technology licensing and development office, which had over a decades' worth of success stories in creating new businesses based on MIT technology. While there, I was responsible for a portfolio of technologies ranging from high-end digital signal processors to image compression and video compression. Because this was 1994, the Internet was really just getting going businesses were just starting to do HTML pages and the like – and as the new kid I was lucky enough to get "anything Internet".

The Wireless Industry

In 1996, I was in a position to finally start my own business because I'd been part of the venture capital community, the entrepreneurial community, and the technology community. In 1996 I started a company called NBX, which stands for network-based exchange. NBX is a business telephone system that competes with traditional PBX systems, but the difference is that it runs entirely over the Internet. We understood that, in order to take advantage of all of the value of the Internet as a communications medium, we needed to make it simple and usable for end users. So we created an Internet telephone, as well as a complete call processing, voice messaging and enhanced services capability using Internet protocol or IP. That was critical to making it easy for users to pick up the phone and get a dial tone. The person making the decision on buying the system saw the value of the Internet. I sold NBX to 3Com in March of 1999 in a very successful sale, and that enabled me, after four months at 3Com, to begin thinking about building the next business. I carried two critical ideas from NBX. One was that the value of the services delivered over the Internet to the telecommunications infrastructure is very high, so I wanted to continue to deliver that kind of value. The second idea was more of a business model concept, in that the greatest value to be achieved in this area is with a carrier-class system, which can support carriers and ISPs as well as the Global 2000 type of enterprise. Providing an outsourced network to enable delivery of enhanced services to the phone was a much stronger business model than the business model that I'd been pursuing at NBX, where we had dedicated hardware and therefore had to sell through a reseller channel. So those two ideas – the business model and the technology –

led to the creation of Informio, and the work that started Informio began in the summer of 1999.

Applicable Skills

First, and most importantly, is understanding technology – not just "how" things work, but how technology is best applied to solve real-world business challenges. That's really been a critical component of my experience as an entrepreneur both at NBX and Informio, and is something I still live and breathe every day. The second, which I picked up while I was practicing law, was the ability to understand the growth cycle of a business, the various transactions, the various players, and the motivation of those players when growing a business, from licensing and commercializing technologies, to raising money, recruiting people, and interacting with Wall Street. At MIT I gained the skill set necessary to start businesses from nothing more than an idea, a technology. I saw a huge range of technology and learned to identify those that had business opportunities associated with them. Frequently in high-tech, technology is created for technology's sake. The reality is that a technology is no good unless there is a business attached to it – technologies should be leveraged for business' sake. That's the important lesson I learned there. I also developed a certain instinct for knowing and understanding when technology opportunities really do have a strong business application. That instinct led to my identifying the segment that I've been working in with NBX and Informio, the intersection of the Internet and the telecommunications industry. That intersection is so exciting because the telecommunications industry has been around for 100 years or more, since the first telephone products were available.

The Internet's been around for a relatively short period of time, and the World Wide Web has really led to the explosion of Internet activity over the last seven years. There are significant cultural and technological clashes between the Internet and the telecom world, and it's that area of turmoil that offers the greatest opportunity for new businesses. That's why it's possible to start businesses like NBX and Informio in a landscape that's currently dotted with the large telecom and datacom equipment vendors, carriers and ISPs.

Coming Attractions in Wireless

From an overall market perspective, the most exciting development that we're going to see is when we no longer think of different devices being associated with different kinds of applications or different kinds of content. So a wireless web device won't just be associated with consumer applications like sports, news, weather, or stock quotes. And a PC won't only be associated with business applications. The reality, and the exciting vision here, is that it is possible to access all Internet content or any intranet content sitting on a web server from any device. So accessing content with your voice via a cell phone, for example, is not a separate initiative, it's an extension of the Internet. The driver from a technological perspective is that, over the next several years, the Internet protocol is going to become the protocol for any device – be it a phone, a Palm computer, or a Blackberry pager. When we reach that point – and it is going to happen relatively quickly – all of these non-PC devices are going to have the multimedia capability of interfacing with Internet content and applications coming from any web server. That's the kind of long-term future that we're headed towards.

Goals for the Wireless World

Wireless will truly "arrive" when people can access the entire Internet from anywhere, anytime. This means accessing and leveraging both audio/voice and data, and overcoming the limits of the existing telephony infrastructure. First generation wireless, or analog cellular, allowed communication via telephone calls, yet the coverage for those calls and the quality of those calls was limited, so doing more was a stretch. The current generation, 2G, has multiple digital standards that provide us with a higher quality user experience for placing and receiving telephone calls, and provides certain types of data-related capabilities. But one of the biggest problems with 2G is that data sessions and telephone sessions cannot co-exist, so we don't really have a multimedia experience. And the wireless text-based data solutions, such as Internet access via the wireless application protocol (WAP), that do exist are of limited quality for several reasons, which I break down into three categories.

The first category is user interface – the limitations of today's wireless telephones are well-documented. Limited screens and limited key pads are compounded by the fact that different permutations exist from Ericsson, Motorola,

The Wireless Industry

Nokia, Samsung, Sanyo, and the like, all with different ways of getting the ampersand to show up on the screen.

The second category is less talked about, but equally important: the user experience. The experience relates to the type of content being accessed. If a Wall Street investment banker wants to put an analyst's report in the hands of his colleague, and it's a PDF file on a server somewhere, receiving that report on a mobile phone's small screen is such a terrible user experience and so inconvenient that it will fail. But think about a user experience where that colleague can receive that analyst's report as streamed audio, so as he is driving to a customer site, he can listen to it as audio in a highly produced manner.

The third category is coverage. The lack of coverage for wireless text can limit a lot of application delivery for the Global 2000. For example, take a Global 2000 enterprise that has a large technical support staff all over the country or perhaps all over the globe. That company may enable its technical support staff to access content using a Palm device. The wireless network that the Palm device uses for exchange of information is of such limited coverage that, in many circumstances, users are just unable to exchange any data.

Those three limitations are further compounded by not being able to include audio and voice interaction. New networks with combined voice and data capabilities, sometimes called 2.5G networks, begin to solve this problem. What I mean by that is a text-based data session can interact with an audio session. Today, on your PC, you can log into a web page that has multimedia, click on an audio report, and have it served up in real streaming media format. The report is in text, you click on it and then you hear it. 2.5G has the potential to enable that kind of interaction as well so you select a piece of data to hear on your phone. That's a step in the right direction. The next step is 3G or 4G or beyond where we actually have the spectrum that can support the bandwidth to talk to multimedia devices, and that will enable us to interact with our phone or our Palm or our Handspring or our Blackberry, and interact with that device for audio and text in a combined session via an IP backbone.

We fundamentally believe that we are ultimately going to a world where the IP of the structure extends all the way to the device. Now we're going to deliver all Internet content and applications sitting on web servers, wherever they may be, to non-PC devices in the same manner that they're accessible from PC devices.

The Impact of Licensing Fees

I think we're seeing licensing fees slow the growth of third-generation wireless in Europe already with some of the spectrum auctions hitting big snags due to cost, among other issues. I think we will see that here in the U.S., and part of the reason is a current lack of vision. Ironically, it's a combination of too much and too little vision all at the same time. The too-much vision piece is all the hype about the wireless Web, because the wireless Web on second-generation platforms today is a poor experience. That hype is driving the extremely high price tag. The too-little vision, though, is the fact that 3G will enable a type of experience that is not limited to the kind of early generation, text-based wireless experiences that we have today, but will expand to a multimedia experience in the future. That kind of multimedia experience (the ability to interface both as text and audio and ultimately even video) will in time justify the value of investment in an IP infrastructure for wireless devices. The trouble is that people are looking at investing in broadband spectrum right now, and they're looking at the applications and are unable to make the economics work. The applications as they sit today are just so feeble that they don't create business models to pay for that bandwidth. But when you realize that audio and voice and other technologies can really expand the value set of those devices in the future, I think the market will begin to realize that value.

3G's Development

If you talk to the device manufacturers and the equipment manufacturers, 3G moving into the mainstream is coming very soon. Nokia and the like have had devices for some time that can operate and provide outstanding incremental functionality for broadband environments, and the other large-scale wireless equipment platform providers would say the same thing. But I think that the current market dynamic – the difficulty in understanding the business model as well as the cost of getting into the business – will slow things down. And I think that's right. The business model should dictate the investment. We shouldn't invest blindly, but count me among the people who believe in the power of IP. The other side of it is that I also believe in the power of the Web experience that we've had over the last seven years. The experience of interfacing with applications either via WAP, WML, or some of the new emerging voice-based applications, doesn't reflect the true potential here. The potential comes from the fact that new standards such as VoiceXML are going to enable applications to be served up from existing Web servers and reach phone devices for voice and audio interaction. And the important point here is that these applications can be developed and served up at Web speed and can be scaled to Web proportions, whereas the WML limitations depend on carriers. WML has promise, but it doesn't really enable Web-speed development of "anytime, anywhere" applications.

Meeting Public Expectations

I think it's possible to get a continuous stream to the Internet over wireless space. But I think that the current expectations are like those in any other burgeoning space. Everything is so hyped that there's risk of short-term disappointment in spite of the strong potential for long-term realization of that vision. The combination of markup languages that really are Internet-based markup languages, the emergence of the broadband IP spectrum promised by 3G networks, and the availability of broadband multi-modal end user devices aren't all in sync yet, but they will be in the next several years.

The Importance of Capital

Funding sources like venture capital are extraordinarily important. Venture capital right now is powering a lot of the innovation in the space, particularly at what you might view as an early phase. For example, the business models that are going to succeed in the wireless industry are those that do two things: provide a solution that overcomes the limitations of today's telephone and Internet, and simultaneously provide an enabling technology and infrastructure for a world where multimedia devices are supported by a network that is a broadband IP network. So that's why I think you're seeing a lot of investments being made right now in infrastructure providers building for that world. The companies that are focused on applications today as the "be all and end all" application will be the road kill of the future.

The Effect of the Markets on Wireless

I think people are realizing that the public markets as an opportunity to raise money or create liquidity are relatively closed and may remain closed for some period of time. So what you need to do in this environment is build up a platform and an infrastructure with a solid business model. The biggest effect of the public market situation today is that, for those companies that have actually received funding, it creates an opportunity to build businesses and business models with less pressure to realize an immediate return on investment via a dangerously overheated stock market. The result is a little bit more of a longer-term horizon for building private companies. Still that long-term horizon is only on the order of three to five years, so it's arguably not that long term a horizon. But that's been the model of the venture capital industry since its inception. This is a five-year process and these are 10-year partnerships as opposed to what we've seen over the 1999-2000 craziness where the time frames were 12 months or less.

Profitability's Role

Profitability is a requirement at this stage.

That's the value of venture capital at early-stage companies, meaning basically start up through product launch. There's an expectation that you do have to invest and build out the infrastructure services and the enabling technologies in order to make the business happen, so there has to be a business model that will generate profitability within the foreseeable horizon. The venture capitalists are valuable because they are willing to make investments early on without immediate profitability. The public market now is disinterested in a business that may be just trying to go public in order to continue to finance itself until it reaches profitability, so business models are everything.

Worldwide Wireless

I think that it's fairly well documented that there's been a much greater uptake in wireless usage for standard placing and receiving of calls in the northern European and Scandinavian countries especially, because of their difference in pricing plans. They've also been the first to experiment with WAP-based technology for text data. Our observation is that they've largely been frustrated with the technology because of the devices and limited bandwidth available today. I think that they are actively looking for alternatives to enable wireless phones, but they're looking at voice and audio technologies as something that provides a better user experience and a better user interface than text. And by leveraging an easily scalable IP infrastructure, they can enable these applications on a global basis.

In the Far East, my take on the success of i-Mode in Japan is that, because the provider has a near monopoly position, they are able to dictate things that just can't be dictated in the U.S. or Europe: the device, the markup language, the price. They've established a business model, and people are forced to pay because the provider has what amounts to a monopoly position. As a result, developers who have applications to build are given incentives to build those applications because they know there's a stream of revenue that they can go out and try to grab. I think that the result is a good model to study because it shows how we can enable an analogous kind of thing to happen here in the U.S. But I think that will ultimately depend on the emergence of broadband-based solutions and applications that can be developed using a Web-style of markup language that everyone agrees upon. We think that VoiceXML and audio and voice interfaces are a much more attractive solution, because there is a single markup language, a single, familiar interface - audio and voice - and there's no issue as to what kind of device to use; all phones will work. So internationally I think there's a lot more activity, but the reason for the activity is very different, especially in Europe. In Europe you're going to see a lot more people experimenting with new things like VoiceXML. In Japan people are going to milk the current monopoly situation for as much revenue as they can.

There are two big problems with the U.S. market. One, we've been slower on the uptake for wireless devices, and the business models in the U.S. are different. The other is that we've been faster on the uptake for Internet types of applications, and the business models on the Internet side have been so severely flawed. The trouble is that in spite of the flaws of the Internet models, which are to give it away for free, acquire customers, and then monetize your customers, those same models are being employed in the case of wireless Internet connectivity in the U.S. So it's like a double whammy effect in the U.S., whereas in Europe and the Far East there may be more traditional emphasis on services for people to pay for. A lot of this business model problem is forcing providers, especially in the U.S., to focus on the enterprise as a customer versus the consumer. In the enterprise, the value proposition that I talked about earlier – extending content and applications to non-PC devices – plays really well because it addresses critical business needs. For example, when a company's workforce is on the road and they need to access their email or other business-critical information, businesses are willing to pay for that immediate access, as evidenced by business models from companies such as Research in Motion, that offers access to corporate email from mobile devices. I think that's where the real business models and the real value propositions are. In the U.S., the problems that I've described have more to do with consumer applications, so I think we're really going to see the most traction among the enterprise.

I'm 100 percent behind the fact that we are going to have an IP-dominated world with multimedia devices that are mobile in everybody's pocket, and there are moves the carriers can make in that direction. There was a recent announcement about AT&T committing to a GSM architecture as a first step toward moving its network to be more capable in the future. I think what's going to need to happen, and maybe will happen in the U.S., is that the carriers are going to need to make the commitment in capital and equipment, as well as investments in spectrum, in order to get that high-bandwidth capability out there. Those that do not make this investment will be penalized in the long run because they lack vision today. Those that have the vision will make the investments and build up those networks for the future, and they will be amply rewarded.

Advice for Startups

For those startups in wireless Internet, the most important thing is to realize that this game is not about wireless per se, it's really about extending the reach of Internet content and applications from Web servers to any non-PC device. When you think in those terms, the equation changes somewhat, and you begin to think in terms of extending applications from existing Web servers and in terms of the markup languages that enable that extension. The other side of it is you need to realize the limitations of today's devices and focus on what can be done with those devices with a high user interface and a high-quality experience. In Informio's case, we're betting on VoiceXML and building tools for companies to rapidly develop applications that extend existing content from their Web servers to reach phones. We're then deploying a network that leverages audio and voice to enable people to use their familiar phones to access and navigate the content. Because we're doing everything in IP, our network will function in the emerging environment – one that that emerges with a full broadband reach all the way down to the end device. My simple advice is that there are too many uncertainties to build a business today that depends on the immediate arrival of a broadband IP world. The more important thing is to think in terms of transitioning to that world as it emerges while at the same time recognizing the limitation of the devices and the network as it stands today.

On Leadership

I think I realized early on that there would be a convergence of telephony and the Internet, and that is what would drive – in large part – the utility of the wireless world. For "wireless" to have meaning, it has to be deployed and used in a way that is meaningful for business, and meaningful on a grander scale than basic phone communication. And the user experience in the wireless realm must be a rich one, or adoption will be limited. I think I'm on the forefront in that regard, while many others in this space either remain in the text world, I know that we are participating in a much larger opportunity, which includes voice and audio interaction. The end result is a rich user experience that is, at the same time, more simple. I have become knowledgeable in this space through the emergence of the Internet protocol as a fundamental communications protocol for both telecom and datacom, and by getting involved with voice over IP and enhanced services over IP to non-PC devices. The logical and most exciting next device as an IP device for voice and enhanced services is the mobile phone, so that's been the path.

Wireless, Ten Years Out

I see us not using the word wireless anymore, for one thing. I think what we're going to see is pervasive, broadband, Internet protocol to every device that we consider an information device. I don't think the world's going to move and merge to a single device, but instead I think we're going to have a fundamental extension of IP and the Internet so that any device becomes an IP device. That will enable just amazing, multimedia applications that we can't even dream up today.

Informio is led by Alex Laats, President, CEO and co-founder. Most recently, Alex was the Chairman, COO and co-founder of NBX Corporation, a manufacturer of business communications systems that operate over data networks, including the LAN and the Internet. NBX Corporation was sold to 3Com Corporation in March 1999 in a $90 million cash transaction. Prior to NBX, Alex was a Technology Licensing Officer at MIT, where he was involved with multiple startup businesses based on MIT technology. Alex started his career as a corporate attorney at Testa, Hurwitz & Thibeault in Boston, where he represented high technology corporations, venture capital funds and investment banks in a variety of transactions.

Inside the Minds

Alex has a JD from Harvard and Physics and Math degrees from MIT.

ROD HOO
===

Reaching the Epitome of Productivity
LGC Wireless
President and CEO

Excitement in Today's Industry

I think the most exciting thing is everybody is talking wireless. Wireless will be expanding people's capabilities to do all kinds of things, changing the way they live and work. There are so many ways in which people can use wireless to improve the quality of life. I like to participate in various activities, and with the ubiquity of wireless capabilities I can be at a non-work related event or venue somewhere and still be able to conduct business. Because of the capabilities of wireless, I'm able to access my home office or communicate with people everywhere, no matter where I am.

Bringing Wireless Into the Mainstream

First of all, the technology has to be a little bit easier to use from a device point of view. The principal application of wireless has been primarily voice communications. More recently there's been the advent of data applications, particularly with the Internet. People want to be able to perform a variety of tasks with their wireless devices, such as continuously checking stock quotes to see how their portfolio is doing. If the manufacturers of these devices and the providers of the network build up the capabilities to make it easier for people to use at the right price, I think it's going to accelerate even faster. I believe the devices currently available and the networks that provide the content and the bandwidth are not quite there yet, but you can see the demand just driving the need for better devices, higher bandwidth and more content.

Using Wireless

I think wireless is really going to enable the paradigm of the virtual office concept. You'll take your desktop with you, via one device if you like using one device where you have voice and data capabilities, or today where you have two devices, the mobile telephone and the PDA. Today, people can only perform certain functions through these devices, but through either a single integrated device or the two that are available now, you can provide a lot of these functions that people want to be able to perform with wireless. One caveat is that the network must be available to provide the capabilities for integration. You must be able to provide and perform these functions when you're on the move, not only when you are away from home in hotel-type environments or convention centers, but when you're physically on the move in a car, airplane or any other truly mobile environment. I think that would be the point at which everyone says, "Ah, now I've reached the epitome of productivity," and that is what I think we're all driving toward.

Challenges Facing Wireless

You have to address that from the point of view of which market you're talking about. In the U.S., for example, I think there are two principal factors. Number one is we do not have a single standard as we have in other parts of the world. In Europe and in many parts of Asia they have standardized on GSM, which has made the availability of services within a country or between countries very, very easy. In the U.S. we have too many standards and it's difficult for people to have true nationwide services. This is a problem that must be overcome. The second factor that I think needs to be changed somewhat is the fact that the U.S., as compared to Europe, has tremendously high-quality wire-line service. The way I used to look at it is that the U.S. has been a little bit behind the rest of the world in adopting wireless services because of the high-quality wire-line services. More recently my thinking has changed in that I believe the reason we've been behind – and we're starting to catch up very fast now – is not so much that wire-line service was good but because the wireless service was bad. As the wireless services start to improve I think you'll see the utilization of the wireless networks increase. Europe has proven this because while the wire-line services are very good there, people are already using many more wireless services because of the availability, and ubiquity, of wireless services.

Challenges Specific to the U.S.

In the U.S. we have multiple air interface protocols. There are at least four or five of them: we use GSM, TDMA, CDMA, iDEN and a plethora of some older analog technologies like AMPS. Many of these networks have been deployed for a very long time. They're very expensive to deploy, and the operators of these networks are still deploying second-generation systems, but they already need to be thinking about third-generation systems because even with second-generation systems the ability to have high-speed data access is not there. That can only come with third-generation systems, which give you the two megabit bandwidth that people really want now. The operators have spent many billions of dollars for the licenses for the spectrum that's been auctioned off by the FCC. Once they've done that, the next big hurdle for them is to spend many more billions of dollars to purchase equipment and deploy networks. Until you can have a network that has a large enough coverage area, it's very difficult to get many subscribers to sign up for your service. That's another major hurdle. In Europe, for example, the standard there is GSM so it's a lot easier. They have inter-country roaming agreements that allow for seamless calling between countries. How they tariff in Europe compared to the U.S. is also a big difference. In Europe the calling party pays, but we have yet to implement that in any really wide scale arrangement here in the U.S. I think those are the hurdles that are not necessarily preventing but are certainly slowing down the growth that one could otherwise expect.

The Potential of Short Messaging Service

Short message service could explode, except that we need to get more bandwidth. Short message service is great for exactly what the name says: short messages. However, people want access to the Internet and browsing type capabilities, so we're going to need a lot more than short message service. The 3G systems must be deployed to provide these capabilities. The other problem in the U.S. is that we are looking at offering 3G systems in the 700 megahertz range and again that's different. Most of the rest of the world is looking at 1900-2100 Megahertz range of frequencies, so again we're going to have an incompatibility of networks providing these kinds of capabilities, and that also means different devices as well.

Broadband Wireless

I think broadband is very important. I think if broadband wireless were available today, you'd see a much higher penetration of users and many more minutes of use than you do now. Again, the fact is that if you want access, you can get email today wirelessly, you can get updates on your stock portfolio, but it's very painful and difficult to use. Getting this on a device that has a graphical user interface with micro-browser type capabilities requires these broadband capabilities, so I think it's very important. It's not a market demand issue, it's a technology availability issue. Many companies are working on this, but the growth of this is slowed because of the different standards in the U.S., limited network capacity, and having to get the price of a hand held device low enough.

The Cost of Building the Wireless Infrastructure

I think the effect of the cost of building the wireless infrastructure is huge. If you look at people who are already utilizing services or are subscribers in existing networks, the demand for capacity on existing networks is growing by leaps and bounds. Providers have to balance how much of their resources they're going to apply to expanding their existing networks – which are second-generation level today – and how much they invest on the third-generation networks for which they've spent billions of dollars acquiring licenses. That's a real challenge. Companies that come up with technology that allows these operators to facilitate network deployments, either expanding capacity in existing first and second-generation networks or facilitating new network build-outs for third-generation services, are going to win because of the high cost of this network build-out.

Convergence of Voice and Wireless

The convergence of voice and wireless is very important. I'm kind of from the old school where I believe the simplest form of input is voice and the simplest form of output is visual. In a mobile environment when you're in your car, voice input really is the only way in which it will be universally adopted because of safety issues. So I strongly believe that when the voice input reaches a high level of accuracy and availability and a low price point, that's going to drive the whole application to such a point that it's going to be a "no-brainer". Everyone's going to want to use it.

Voice is an enabling technology for input, but it's not really an application. And it is probably the most important input technology. Then you have to look at the whole spectrum of things from the access highway. You have to have technology that allows users to have access no matter where they are. Thus, access is needed in the inner regions of a city canyon, on the top floor of a 100-story building, or throughout urban tunnels. People will not tolerate dropped calls anymore, particularly as they move to using the wireless device as their principal mode of communication. These are all infrastructure-type things that must be there before all these wonderful content applications will take off. Without the infrastructure reaching the point of say, 98 percent coverage in any given area, the location-based applications that are being talked about quite a bit are not going to be utilized as much as they could be.

Government Regulation

One of the problems with the government is that the spectrum that's been allocated for wireless in third-generation networks is in the 700 Megahertz range. That's different from the spectrum that's being allocated in the rest of the world. I think that's an area that needs to be revisited somehow. Also, there has been relatively little spectrum allocated for other uses. Outside of that, I think the government should just let the industry pretty much run on its own rather than playing Big Brother. I think that the wireless industry has companies that are well managed from a service-provider point of view. We have many companies that can develop great applications, and I think the government should not regulate them too much, and just allow the market to drive some of these capabilities.

Protecting Privacy

Certainly with things like location-based services and GPS, people knowing or having the capability to figure out where you're at is an issue of privacy and security. But there's another side as well. There are many documented cases where people had their cell phones turned on, got into trouble, and were able to get the kind of help they needed.

Device Evolution

People like big screens, but if I take myself and my close circle of friends as an example, we still like it small enough that we can stick it into our pocket. Then if you have a big screen, you also require power. For me, the device must fit into my pocket or on my belt, which precludes a very large screen. Wireless really is targeted for the mobile person, and while the mobile person would love to have a big screen, I think they would sacrifice the big screen for lightness or length of battery power and things like that.

Consumer Choices

I think the options will increase dramatically in the near future. Asia is an example with i-Mode capability in Japan. A heavy percentage of the I-mode users are the young set, the teenagers who are not looking at the business-type applications at all but are looking at it more for entertainment purposes. Then you have the business people, the more traditional ones who want to access not only voice communications and voice mail but also email and their calendar. In my opinion, the "killer applications" for business are email, calendaring and directory. I think you'll see devices that will be optimized for these different sets of users in the different segments of the market.

Breaking In

I think the barriers to entry are very high on the infrastructure side, but the barriers to entry from an application side are still relatively low. I think you'll see more related to software, and these people will be developing wireless applications to market to the service providers to offer to their end users. I think the new set of players coming into the wireless space will be the non-traditional telecom players such as the companies that have the access, the rights or the assets, whether it is buildings, wire-line fiber networks, or other kinds of infrastructure that can be applied as either backbone for the wireless networks or act as building blocks for wireless systems to facilitate wireless network deployment. Building owners and property management companies are starting to recognize the value of the asset that they hold: the rooftops where you can put up antennas or base stations, or the building where you can deploy wireless networks. These are becoming extremely valuable commodities as node foundations in a network. In the past they leased these things out to providers and tower builders at relatively low rates, but now I think they're demanding a lot higher return for this access.

Coming Together

I think there will definitely be consolidation. Right now there are a lot of players out there and a lot of new players at different levels. From the service provider level, there are already mergers and joint ventures between big, big players. Witness what happened in the U.S. with Verizon recently. And that's also going on in Europe with the new third-generation licenses that have just been auctioned. New players are coming on the scene. Some of the new players don't know how they take that quantum leap to build out that network. One of the ways is to buy an existing provider that perhaps is not operating as profitably as it could. I think you're going to see a lot of that happening over the next few years. When you look at truly global services, more consolidations will occur due to simple economic reasons. And then you take it a next level down to the applications. Already we've had a lot of companies making acquisitions to add to their portfolio of wireless applications. There are also many small companies that are starting to develop not only applications but standard protocol stacks for the applications. I think you're going to see not only the horizontal integration and mergers but some vertical integration as well.

A Path to Profitability

Historically you look at software value-added applications as being very, very profitable, but I think that with the growth in the bandwidth and capacity requirements, those companies or providers that can supply high bandwidth to the users will have very profitable models as well.

Wireless Winners

From a provider point of view – I think you always start there – I think they've got to offer coverage for the footprint for which their licenses have been purchased. If they have enough coverage, then they have to have enough capacity. They have to have enough bandwidth to satisfy their users, because they're going to demand a lot more bandwidth to access all these bandwidth-intensive applications. So you start with coverage, then you provide capacity, and then applications. Above all, the integrity of the networks must be maintained to the highest level so it will prevent or minimize users from churning to a competing service provider. That's where it all starts. And then the vendors providing technology or applications to the service providers that can best understand the challenges of these operators and best meet their needs, will be the winners.

A Vision for the Industry

Our vision for this industry is that we are clearly focused on creating the best high-quality broadband solutions to essentially allow people to expand the reach of their wireless services. So we want to provide broadband access, anytime, anywhere – particularly to users on the move. Our particular challenge is to get the operators to truly understand that there are many users who really put a high value on access inside structures and facilities. Today many of the service providers, especially the newer ones, are focused on building out the macro network. But if you look at the density of the users in buildings, you'll find that there are many additional minutes of use that could be captured if the service providers would really focus on providing coverage and capacity to the highest degree there. I think that is our challenge to work with the providers and to meet these particular needs.

Keys to the Future

First, there is the user interface. You have to get to the point where the consumers will be able to use these devices to access both voice and data services conveniently and at the right price point. Voice input, the size of the device and providing coverage anytime, from anywhere are critical attributes. From the network side, I think seamless integration or seamless connectivity to the application, whether for business or personal services, is important. The network must provide adequate response time bandwidth to satisfy the growing number of users and their increasing requirements.

Rod has more than 25 years experience in telecommunications systems marketing, development, and operations. He served most recently as general manager, international business development and marketing for the Octel Messaging Division of Lucent Technologies. Previously, he was vice president of product development at Centigram Communications, and director of business communications development at Bell Northern Research/Nortel. Rod received his MSEE and BSEE from the University of Hawaii and his MBA from Santa Clara University.

SCOTT BRADNER
Identifying Revenue Opportunities
Harvard University
Senior Technical Consultant

Issues Facing the Wireless Industry

I think the major issue is the methods of return on investment. It's very hard to see. This isn't a technical issue, it's a business issue, so it's very hard to see how the wireless world is actually going to make its money. Particularly because of the investment in the wireless spectrum auctions, it's a very, very large investment for a questionable rate of return. Some countries like Switzerland seem to have much lower rates of investment simply because they're a one-to-one match between the number of bidders and the number of licenses, but where there's not, there has been huge payments, particularly in Great Britain and Germany and potentially here in a couple of years. But this is at the same time as they move toward end-to-end Internet type connectivity for all IP networks in 3G, for example, which cut out the middle man or the carrier for revenue. So I think these are going to be some extremely difficult times coming up in the area of paying for the infrastructure that people are putting in.

Wireless Readiness

I don't think that most of the world is ready. Japan has shown that you can do a lot with toys, and some of the biggest services on i-Mode are toys, downloadable cartoon characters, karaoke or things like that, but it's got a remarkable penetration. How well that translates to the rest of the world I don't know. The experience so far with WAP has been very disappointing, partially because of performance, partially because of price, and partially because of functionality. People just don't get what they think they're paying for when they're buying these types of services. So I'm not sure that we're ready in terms of the consumers not having applications. I think they are there, checking your stocks is only one thing. Mostly teenagers doing instant messaging has turned out to be an absolutely phenomenal service on the wired market, and there's no reason why it wouldn't be on the wireless market, but the carriers and the providers have not internalized what they can and cannot get away with. For example, the idea that location-dependent advertising: wanting my phone to ring to say that I'm passing the Starbucks, which seems to be a dream of many of the carriers, I think is totally demented. First of all, I don't like coffee, and second of all, I wouldn't want to know.

Making Money

The only revenue-generating area I can see wireless companies capitalizing on is minutes of air time. If I got IP connectivity, which I believe is necessary, then the carrier actually can't control who I talk to unless it uses something like a WAP gateway, but WAP has not shown to be successful and even there the French courts have told France Telecom that they can't require one of their customers to use a France Telecom WAP gateway; they have to let the customer select a third-party gateway if they want to. And if that's the case, France Telecom doesn't get the gateway revenues or anything other than minutes of air time, so I don't see that they can get anything but minutes of air time. And I worry that this is a commodity environment and driven by the stupidest vendor, the one that's willing to cut prices in order to get market share, or publicity, or impress the stock market, and winds up driving down the prices for everybody. This is the airline model where some airline decides to cut prices and the rest follow them into a crash dive.

The Importance of Capital

Funding is absolutely critical for technology. I don't know how long it's going to last in the carrier support side. I'm on the advisory board for Malibu Networks, which is doing work in the wireless space. Venture capital funding and the stock market are absolutely critical. It's not something you go off to banks for, though I was approached by a large bank, making sure that I would know that they were a venture firm now. It's been an amazing run of the last half dozen years or so where the investment money has been there to be able to support a number of these activities. Many of them aren't going to make it, but the ones that do can be very dramatic.

A Path to Profitability

I don't think the push for profitability is unique. I think the last stock market cycle has been a real wake-up call to the venture community. The venture community had 10 years ago been in the market where there wasn't that many VCs. They expected that maybe half the companies they funded wouldn't exist in a few years and only one out of ten would make it big. They then had a cycle where as many as half the companies they funded made it big, and this was a real change in the concept of what funding was all about. It brought much, much more money into the market. There are a number of funds right now that are multi-billion dollar funds.

Worldwide Wireless

Certainly in Europe we've got relatively few standards and I think it will stay that way. Japan is Japan. China has political reasons to be independent and may go its own way or may not; it's hard to tell at this point but they are somewhat of a sizeable market growing faster than the rest of the world combined. The U.S. has traditionally been fragmented. It's not been good for us. The multi-lingual, in the sense of technology, chips that Motorola and others are putting out have rescued us a little bit, but still it's really ridiculous. This is an area where it may be a little too lax as far as standardization goes. I'm not somebody who is in favor of government setting standards because I think in general they set the wrong ones too slowly, but I find it difficult to believe that it's in the industry's interest to have three or four standards on how you do wireless.

The U.S. certainly is different from Europe and Asia. The population density patterns are very different, and the coverage patterns are very different. In Western Europe and

Japan, the population densities are far higher, so it doesn't take anywhere near the infrastructure investment to get reasonable coverage, whereas that's not the case here. The distances are much larger. There's a story that says some of the European car makers didn't understand why the U.S. customers were so insistent on having cup holders in their cars, because in Europe you hardly drive long enough that you need a cup holder and in the U.S. you can't imagine not having one. And I think that's the case with wireless. You've got space where even today with the coverage, with the rather large investment that's been made, it's spotty coverage for the existing wireless world. The existing cell-phone world is very spotty, and when you're talking about next generation and after that, 3G, it's going to be very, very large investments. The idea that we can continue in this mode of having multiple carriers and multiple technologies putting towers up beside each other is just not going to make it. I think the community pressure is going to push back on that to the level where there's got to be some consolidation, whether it's in a common-carrier type tower system where somebody builds a tower and anybody can use them or some industry consolidation around standards.

Industry Players

It's a difference between the carriers and the suppliers. Of the suppliers, certainly Ericsson and Nokia are the major ones, and I don't see any particular reason to think that they won't be. Each of those has recently shown adoption of their technology in some important space. The picture of the Qualcomm president talking to the president of China is an interesting one for the investment community. Folks say that during the gold rush no gold miner made money, the only ones who made money were the ones who made shovels and pans, and we're in the market where those companies are doing a pretty good job of building shovels. Ericsson has some very interesting phones coming up that are targeted for a wireless Internet world, and in particular they recognize that if they're going to be very successful, they need to get in the mode where people want to buy fancier phones. We've got a lot of Nokia phones but also a lot of third-party phones that are very generic. People don't make a great deal of money off of any particular phone, whereas Ericsson's model as seen by the phone that they introduced recently with a large touch-screen display on it, recognizes that the way to drive the adoption of new phones is to make the phone something that can be programmed – that you can download a Java applet to and put a new application on it. This is just like the PC market where Microsoft will ensure that people need to get bigger and better PCs to just keep the software doing the same thing it used to do. And that's going to happen in the phone world too, and Ericsson's the only one I've seen actually doing this today who understands that the phone is an instrument that third parties can program.

Challenges to the Wireless Industry

Licensing is a very big one. Spending $1600 per potential customer where a customer is defined as 60 percent of the population, which is what was done in England and Germany, is unlikely to ever be paid back. So if licensing is done at that rate, I think it will stop dead any kind of deployment. The same thing is true in the U.S. The estimates of $180 billion for licenses in 2002, when the next auction happens, to me, just stifle the deployment. People who bought those licenses could not afford to then put out the infrastructure to make use of them and it would kill it. I'm a fan of dealing with unlicensed or minimally licensed bands and spread-spectrum kinds of solutions. People are experimenting with 802.11 in marinas and airports and things like that. It's the wrong technology to do it with, but that's the stuff that the license lets you do it with, and it works pretty well. I'd like to see more unlicensed bands where there's regulation on transmitter power, and if that happens, I think we'll have an explosion of use because putting in the infrastructure will be the major piece of the cost of the licenses and you get directly paid back on that. But if licenses stay too high, there's going to be a considerable damping effect. Standards are a problem. Without some kind of consolidation in the standards space at the base level, then we've got a problem. In the IETF we're worrying about doing seamless mobility, but that's at the IP layer and above, and I think we're going to have some good standards in that space so that you can take your Palm VII and move it to the wireless world from the wireline world and have it continue to operate without any glitches or interruptions in the performance. In that kind of space I think we're doing okay, the standards organizations are all working in various aspects of the higher level of standards for Internet service over the wireless world. The lower level, the GSM versus CDMA, etc., I think we're not doing well at all.

Bringing Wireless Into the Mainstream

The problem is we're having a hard time figuring out how to make things easy. The industry in general, technology in general, seems to be genetically incapable of making things simple. How many people have 12:00 blinking on their VCRs? It shouldn't be hard to set a clock in a VCR, and yet it's made almost impossible. I think that's one of the things we've seen some history of in the WAP space. The service that's being provided is stuff that people find very complicated and very clumsy to use. It seems like there was no human factors person within half a continent of some of these providers when they came up with these systems. I think there's going to have to be a lot of thinking about how to give good interaction over the small display space that you have on most cell phones. The Ericsson phone with a larger display has some advantages but it's still very small. They're still going to have to do a lot of work in ergonomics in figuring out just how to interact with this sort of thing. But once it's done, I suspect we'll do pretty well, and in particular, if we get deployment of the things like that Ericsson Java-based phone, we're going to have a lot of third parties, not just the carriers, but third parties being able to experiment and figure out if they can give you a better way to interact with the environment with better services and the like. If we're stuck with the WAP model of relatively few service providers, then there's a problem. i-Mode has shown that opening up the service platform and letting the gazillion third parties provide services is a very successful market, a very successful ploy, but I don't see the equivalent understanding here with the U.S. carriers.

Consumer Use

I suspect that it'll wind up that the big initial push will be for short messages, called instant messaging in the AOL space, but just short messages. They have turned out to be extremely popular. There are some of these messaging services already running in Europe. They have proved to be unbelievably popular and even collecting a penny a message, which isn't very much if it's billed properly through the phone system, can be an extremely profitable space and one where we've seen adoption rates that are just unbelievable, teenagers talking to 20 friends at once over instant messaging and the charge goes on daddy's bill. I think that's going to be a huge success. In a relatively confined population, it's the teenager-type population, it's expanding into business but not anywhere near the level of adoption. After we grow through a spate of this kind of service and the kind of toy services that have shown to be popular, whether it's downloading cartoon characters or different ringing tones or karaoke, we'll start to get some serious services, and they're going to probably be some of the location-dependent services where you can query to find the closest coffee rather than it tells you. I don't think that's ever going to be a success. I think people would drop the service in milliseconds of being subjected to calls when they didn't ask for them, in addition to the privacy worries of Starbucks knowing where you are, so I think there's going to be location-dependent services where you poke in the phone saying I'm hungry, steak, and it will tell you what's around. That kind of thing, I suspect, is going to be successful once the user interface is worked out. It will be the kind of thing that the average consumer would want, walking around New York City it would have been nice to be able to find out just where something was and that it was in the upper third of the class of restaurants.

Device Interface

The thing that is amazing is there is instant messaging that's used in Europe and the wireless space. The interface on that turns out to be incredibly awful, but it's phenomenally popular. So I think if the service is right they'll overcome the interface, I'm not sure for how long, but they'll overcome the interface. If you think back at kids and Pokemon, how many Pokemon characters there are and the 4-year-old kids know them and the history of all of them and they can deal with complexity, so I don't think they're going to have a problem with a relatively complicated interface. Their mothers and fathers at home may have a lot of trouble, but the kids will do just fine. So in order to keep those kids as they grow up, we're going to have to do better human factor stuff. It's not going to be easy. I don't think we're going to have people muttering at their phones as the common mode. I don't think voice recognition is going to be the killer interface. I think it's going to be a well-designed, touch-sensitive screen.

Protecting Privacy

There are a number of privacy issues. The obvious one is location sensitivity. A current wireless world tracks the user at some level of granularity. It's not terribly great – but in some places they can get you within 100 feet and in some places it's within a few hundred feet. The stuff that the FBI tried to insist on, which did signal strengths in the various cells, would get you down within tens of feet. The courts have overturned that as my understanding goes, so there's a little less worry there, but here is a situation where the carrier has a database of wherever you've been when the phone's on, years of data potentially. Let's say you get into a messy divorce, and maybe your soon-to-be-ex-wife would like to know where you've been every day, every minute for the last year. This could get a little invasive, and at the moment it's not clear at what level of authority police have to request it, but it does not appear that they need a court order or a subpoena. They can just knock on the door and ask for it, so there's a worry there.

The worry gets worse if somehow the carrier gets advertisers involved – such as Starbucks figuring out you're walking by a store. That gets to be a serious privacy issue. Then there's the issue of being overheard. It's relatively easy to put an encryption in but it's not clear that governments will permit that to occur, because if you do that, you can't wire tap, and this is a concern on the part of the FBI and other government police agencies in other countries. England is proposing ISPs keep forever all emails that you send. Other than location sensitivity, I'm not sure there's a great deal of special privacy issues with the wireless space, but there's an awful lot of privacy issues with the IP connectivity, with wire tapping being a major one.

Government Regulation

I don't believe in government standards. I was a witness for the American Library Association during the Communications Decency Act trial. At one point, one of the Justice Department lawyers asked me, "Couldn't the government set the standards to do something?" That particular trial was to label traffic, label your messages in ways that they could determine whether this was something a 17-year-old should see or not. Before I got a chance to answer one, of the judges asked me something that translated into, "But don't government-mandated standards inhibit innovation?" And they do. The government tried to insist on the OSI protocol, and it stifled for quite a while the innovation that the Internet has shown. The Internet has shown a great deal of innovation because the standards are very straightforward. Almost all of the standard parts are some very low level parts. IP itself, TCP itself, and things sitting on top of them are not standard, so you or your friend can create a new protocol, a new Web, and people can adopt it without having to worry about getting permission from the carrier. I fear that if the government starts setting standards, particularly at the higher levels, then we're in for some serious problems of innovation and we're not going to see the kind of dynamic explosion of applications and uses that the Internet had shown.

On the other hand, I fear the fragmentation that a lack of standardization leads to. One of the issues in the AOL/Time Warner merger talks was over standardization of instant messaging and how companies like that can fragment the market. This is potentially a very serious concern. I don't think the government should set the standard for instant messaging, for example, but I think it should insist that large carriers in the position to dominate be compatible with a standard or can gateway to the standard. At the lower layers of wireless, I can understand why there's reluctance to set a standard but the lack of standards has hurt us. The coincidence of standards in Europe has helped them, and I'm not sure that we can afford the luxury in the

U.S. of continuing to let that sort of stuff fly. The same sort of thing in HDTV – the government did not set a standard for it – and I think that's hurt the industry tremendously. So I think that the government needs to be involved in adopting a standard – not creating a standard – but adopting a standard at some very base levels.

Killer Apps

Toys are the killer apps so far. It's just that the toys are things. They got 1.6 million subscribers to something that downloads cartoon characters to your cell phone. Now who would of thunk? I would have never possibly imagined that, and yet it's there, it's a cheap service – less than $1 a month – the billing costs don't kill the vendor, but it's that sort of thing that has proven to be popular, much more popular than instantly getting stock updates. There's a lot of revenue in toys it seems, and there's a lot of pull for it, so I think the killer apps are things that most businesses would not consider serious. It may migrate into significant revenue for things that business would consider to be serious, like stock market tracking or news tracking or business-level instant messaging, but I think that the initial stuff is going to be quirky little things that third parties figure out, like the pet rock of the wireless space.

Making Money in the Wireless Space

One, do service in a place where you didn't have to pay billions of dollars for your license. Second, realize that what you're in the business of delivering is good interconnection. You're not going to be in the business of intermediating between the customer and the service, so for the IP side and for the data side, the carrier should be transparent and be selling minutes of air time. The carriers that go in there and think they're going to run a gateway that they're going to charge you differently based on what type of traffic you're sending are going to start losing business. They're going to put a lot of infrastructure in and find out that they're not getting a return for that infrastructure. The bottom line: I think the biggest area of profitability for the carrier is going to be in billing. The billing for third-party services, such as done by DoCoMo, can be very profitable without doing much work. For example, the cartoon folks with 1.6 million subscribers send their bills through the DoCoMo normal billing structure and DoCoMo takes 9 percent. They get bulk billing information, and it's included in the regular bills. So I think that the biggest money is going to be minutes and billing. As for billing for third parties, I doubt very much that many carriers are going to be able to provide services that are generally useful enough or confineable enough that they're going to make money at it. By confineable enough, I mean there's no reason I have to use Verizon's instant message gateway or instant messaging server. If Verizon tries to rip me off for using their instant messaging server, I will use a third party's. So where as Verizon can not make money billing me for the instant messages I send from using that third party gateway, I don't think they're going to make much money providing that service themselves or, more particularly, trying to lock me into using their service.

Business models will ultimately decide who wins in wireless. I think that a business model that understands that the carrier is not going to find the killer app, and facilitating third parties selling the killer app when they find it will be the carriers that are going to make money. The ones that think they know it all, think they know what all of their customers' desires are and try and lock them in, they're going to lose market share and they're simply going to lose money. It's going to be too expensive for them to set up the infrastructure for too little return. The revenue sources are carriers helping other third parties to provide services.

Innovation in the Wireless Industry

I suspect that the technology stuff is going to trail off, because there aren't that many new fundamental technologies in the wireless space. Once you've defined what the basic carriage is, there are optimizations: how to build a slightly better base station that's more efficient, that doesn't take as much power, is a little bit smaller, and how to build a head that can talk to more base stations. Those are incremental changes and there's certainly going to be some activity there, but I don't think there is going to be biggies. I think where the innovation's going to happen is in the services. The difficultly in the venture world is that the venture capital people don't like to fund software companies, so I think that the investment in the wireless space is going to diminish. The basic technologies will be done and the place where the money could be used isn't the space where the VCs seem to be comfortable.

Corporate Future

I think there will be continued consolidation in the carrier space. That seems to be the way of the world these days. In the applications services space, I don't think so. I think that we'll see that it is the quirky little service, the karaoke service that is unaffiliated with the carrier, that's going to make money. One of the things about the Internet that people don't really get that well, and I think it's an important feature, is that this end-to-end model, this model of where my application talks to your application or my cell-phone client talks to a server that you can put up or your next door neighbor can put up or the carrier can put up. As long as the network between those is transparent and carries the data, this provides a rich environment for doing experimentation. Carrier-based or core-based services don't tend to innovate very well in that it's disruptive to put in a new piece of technology. If you're going to do something that changes everybody's email system, you're going to do it very carefully and you're going to take years of planning and you've got to be really convinced it's a good thing to do. But if I can download a Java applet to change my email interface and use somebody else's server instead of yours, I can do that easily. It's easy to innovate. This is relatively unimportant in an environment where you understand what the customer wants. Historically in voice service we've understood what the customer wants; it's been developed over 100 years that we've got a 12-button keypad and everything works off that, and when you go to Verizon and say you want voice service you pretty much know what you're going to get. You may get a few features like call waiting or call forwarding, but fundamentally you know what you're going to get. When Verizon wants to add a new feature like *69 it can take a very long time.

But we don't know what the customer wants in this wireless space or even in the Internet space in general. In the wireless space in particular, we don't know what the customer is going to want when we talk about Internet-enabled cell phones, Internet-enabled mobile phones. We don't know because we have never experimented. We don't know what the definition of voice service for the wireless space is going to be in two years. That wireless may include directory services, IP-enabled directory services, a local map, query for the local Starbucks, any number of things that we just don't know. We don't know what the user interface is, we don't know what the services will turn out to be, and in an environment where we don't know who the people are going to be, the winners are the ones that come up with them. They're not likely to be the carriers, they're likely to be third parties that can experiment easily. Now in an Internet end-to-end world, they can experiment easily. When you win, you win big. In a Harvard graduate student's Ph.D. thesis, he uses the real options theory of economics to show that in an environment of high market uncertainty, it is very advantageous to be able to do lots of experiments. Many of those experiments will fail, but the ones that succeed are likely to be the market dominators, so they succeed very big. If there's low market uncertainty, you know exactly what the customer wants and it drives it to a commodity market. If everybody is doing the same thing then you're competing with somebody doing the same thing, and how do you compete? You beat them on the basis of price, whereas if you're competing on the basis of idea, you can compete on the basis of function.

Keys to the Future

Assuming all the other stuff is neutral, such as pay for the licenses and a reasonable adoption of standards, the biggest thing is the understanding within a carrier of the role of a carrier. A wireless carrier to date has completely owned the customer. An Internet service provider, not AOL but a regular Internet service provider like CompuServe, doesn't own the customer. They're a conduit for the customer, and the customer goes someplace else for services. When carriers understand that and that they need to facilitate third parties' value, such as doing billing for third parties, I think they are going to be very successful. The ones that don't understand it, the ones that think they're going to capture the customer and exclude others to provide services for them will fail. So the biggest issue is whether the carrier can understand that the business is different in the Internet. The business is one of carriage, which is where the title comes from, rather than one of capture.

Scott Bradner has been involved in the design, operation and use of data networks at Harvard University since the early days of the ARPANET. He was involved in the design of the Harvard High-Speed Data Network (HSDN), the Longwood Medical Area network (LMAnet) and NEARNET. He was founding chair of the technical committees of LMAnet, NEARNET and CoREN.

Mr. Bradner is the codirector of the Transport Area in the IETF, is a member of the IESG, and until June 1999 was an elected trustee of the Internet Society where he still serves as the Vice President for Standards. He was also codirector of the IETF IP next generation effort and is coeditor of

"IPng: Internet Protocol Next Generation" from Addison-Wesley and is member of the Wiley Network Council.

Mr. Bradner is a senior technical consultant at the Harvard Office of the Provost, where he provides technical advice and guidance on issues relating to the Harvard data networks and new technologies. He founded the Harvard Network Device Test Lab, is a frequent speaker at technical conferences, a weekly columnist for Network World, an instructor for Interop, and does a bit of independent consulting on the side.

TOM MOORE
The Wireless Satellite Space
WildBlue
President and CEO

Excitement in the Wireless Space

There are lots of interesting things going on in the wireless satellite space. First and foremost, a two-way wireless satellite broadband connection will revolutionize the home of the future. The broadband home of the future will offer everything from multi-media entertainment to home management and security. It will enable remote, interactive classroom participation and allow telecommuters to be tied much more closely to their co-workers. I get excited about the changes it will make in a lot of peoples' lives. I also get excited about the technological innovations that are making these new applications possible. Revolutionary changes in digital signal processing, new kinds of modulation techniques, forward error correction, and performance enhancing proxies to adapt to a high latency environment are all clever innovations that create a high performance system for delivering very rich broadband content to the home. I also get excited about a slightly overused term – convergence. Combining the high quality video and audio you see on TV with the two-way interactivity of a broadband connection will create a new user experience that we think will be more compelling than the experience one currently gets even with a DSL or cable modem high speed connection.

Tomorrow in Wireless

The wireless satellite broadband revolution will begin to make its mark within the next year or two. Demand for broadband in general is exploding, over 5 million homes have broadband connections and the growth rate is pretty steep. For large portions of the country, satellite broadband will be the only practical way to satisfy the demand for broadband. Right now monthly service via satellite broadband is close to double the price of cable modem or DSL which is probably limiting appeal to some extent. By next year, we expect the price of satellite broadband service will be comparable to what consumers are paying for cable modem or DSL today, so we think that you will see the revolution begin to take shape within the next couple of years. The other factor that could drive the demand for broadband is the development of exciting new applications. Just as new software applications drive the demand for high performance computers, new bandwidth intensive applications could encourage Internet users to upgrade to a high-speed connection. I think we are in the infancy of the development of broadband applications that will make a high-speed connection to the Internet a "must have".

Challenges to Wireless

We believe that affordable pricing and the low cost platform that enables it is a key challenge for our industry. Satellite service has existed for years, but the equipment is expensive and the service fees are high.

The second challenge is access to capital. Many telecommunications programs, including satellite programs, are capital intensive. You need to spend money up front to build the infrastructure and then wait for the subscriber base to grow to generate a return. Attracting capital to these kinds of programs is getting more difficult. The flip side to that is that limited availability of capital can help to prevent the market from becoming overbuilt.

The third challenge is finding the right talent. The market is very tight for people who know a lot about satellite communications, the Internet and the development of a world-class customer service operation.

The biggest challenge to two-way broadband is affordability of the service and the equipment. Once affordable service is available to virtually any home or business in the continental U.S., we believe there will be a lot to be excited about.

Satellite services today use existing Ku-band satellites that were designed for broadcast applications and not optimized for broadband applications. As a result, they have a relatively high cost per user when these broadband applications are supported. The next generation Ka-band spot beam satellite architecture increases capacity dramatically by utilizing multiple spot beams that simultaneously transmit different data streams to different users. This increases capacity and reduces the cost per user dramatically.

We are also very aggressive about reducing the cost of the equipment at the user's home. From my experience in cable, I know that cable modem penetration did not take off until the cost of the equipment dropped to an affordable level. The creation of a standard, low cost platform (DOCSIS) helped drive the costs where they needed to be. We believe that a similar approach, modified for some of the unique aspects of satellite transmission, will give us the lowest cost modem because it uses high volume, low cost components. Cable modems are providing broadband connectivity to millions of homes, so we didn't see a need to reinvent that wheel and start from scratch. We want to start from a known low cost base and only add or modify technology as necessary for the satellite environment.

Industry Standards

We believe that the establishment of standards is very important to the industry. Standards drive scale economies and efficiencies and they foster rapid technology development. Proprietary designs usually require lower volume, higher-priced components. Since affordability is such an important factor for consumers, we believe standardization is the right way to go. We want to take this one step further by applying the standards from related industries – cable modem and satellite TV – so that satellite broadband can benefit from the high volume low cost components used by those industries.

The Importance of Markets and Money

I think it's very important because these are capital-intensive industries. There is lots of precedent for capital markets funding the development of industries that required up front investment to build the infrastructure. Many of the high growth telecom companies, from cellular to satellite TV, invested billions of dollars raised in public markets and have generated attractive returns for investors. We believe that companies developing next generation satellite broadband will be attractive investment opportunities because they are well positioned: 1) they will offer speeds up to 50 times faster that dial up connections; 2) they will have broader geographic coverage than DSL or cable modem service; and 3) they will have a lower cost structure than existing Ku-band satellite services. We believe that sponsorship by the right strategic investors is critical for the public markets to feel excited about a particular program as well.

The Cost of Building the Wireless Infrastructure

First of all, the infrastructure cost for last mile connectivity via satellite in the ex-urban markets is a fraction of the cost of reaching those homes through terrestrial means. Second, the investment to date is not that significant. The demand for broadband is growing rapidly and it will require a lot of capacity to meet the needs of the millions of homes and businesses that the analysts predict will want to subscribe to broadband services. There are very few next generation broadband satellites under construction. If anything, it makes sense for the pace of investment to pick up in order to keep up with the projected demand. Companies that bring capacity online early should expect robust demand.

A Path to Profitability

We believe that providing broadband access via satellite will be profitable for companies with the low cost structure of a next generation satellite broadband system. The rapid growth of broadband subscribers, the absence of cable modem and DSL competitors and the cost advantage versus existing Ku-band services should allow for attractive economics. We also believe that portal revenues from exciting broadband applications under development could be significant. Very bright people are working on concepts like music subscription services, video-on-demand and broadband enhanced shopping on the web. Internet service providers often earn a share of the e-commerce spending of their subscribers in the form of portal revenues or online advertising fees.

New Players

Creation of new startups is hard to predict. On the one hand, we think the market opportunity is sizable. On the other hand, access to orbital slots and ability to raise capital in a tougher market presents significant barriers to entry. The lead-time to build and launch a satellite system – up to three years – could also be a deterrent to a startup in this environment.

Piecing Together Satellite and Wireless

The two major segments in wireless broadband connectivity are satellite and terrestrial wireless, which uses transmission towers that use multi-channel multipoint distribution service (MMDS) or local multi-point distribution service (LMDS) technologies. WorldCom and Sprint PCS have acquired several MMDS operators and have announced their intention to use this spectrum to provide broadband Internet access. In addition, other operators, such as WinStar Communications Inc. and Advanced Radio Telecom Corp., intend to offer broadband Internet access to business customers. Satellite service has virtually ubiquitous coverage, so population density is not an issue. Both MMDS and LMDS need enough customers within sight of a tower to justify the cost of the tower. Areas with higher population density have more potential customers, but also have a greater likelihood of competition from DSL or cable modem service. So we believe there is a place for satellite connectivity especially in low population density areas where investment in terrestrial wireline and wireless services will be limited.

Killer Satellite Apps

Well obviously satellite TV is a killer app. With almost 15M subscribers in the US today and growing at an astronomical pace people are quite comfortable putting a small dish on their roof to receive multi-channel video programming. We believe there may be similar demand for broadband Internet access via satellite as well. We think that broadband will enhance popular Internet applications that exist today and enable new ones that are simply not possible over a narrowband connection. In the first group, popular applications like email can be enhanced with richer content – digital home video attachments, etc. Web surfing and the news and information on the web will benefit from better quality video and audio. Essentially, it will be the convergence of the high quality you see on TV with the interactivity a broadband connection makes possible. Satellites are great at delivering huge amounts of content (data, video, audio) directly to the home in a seamless way.

We can only imagine the new applications that will be developed to take advantage of a broadband connection. With over 50 million people using Napster, it is apparent that moving music audio around is pretty cool. Receiving software or media rich games or videos over a broadband connection also seems compelling. A broadband connection combined with a satellite broadcast connection into a home gateway with gigabytes of storage will enable all kinds of new applications and services. This combined with personalization might virtually remove the need to procure electronic media any other way. Many companies are working on killer applications that will require signing up for broadband service. We don't plan to be experts in the applications development space. We plan to be experts in providing the lowest cost, reliable, ubiquitous, high-speed connection to the Internet. Of course, we will focus on ease-of-use and top-notch customer service as well.

Satellites Worldwide

We pride ourselves in the United States as being innovators in the telecommunications world. The Internet more or less got started here, the best software companies are here, and even some of the more creative telecommunications providers are here. A majority of most of the compelling programming and content is created here as well. In the satellite world, however, some of the most important innovations have occurred outside the U.S. One example is B Sky B, which is a News Corp. service. It's basically the equivalent of Direct TV or Echostar over Europe. They have rolled out interactive TV services much more aggressively than their U.S. counterparts. B Sky B has several million interactive customers that are ordering a pizza on the television, looking down different camera angles at sporting events, looking up sports scores when they're watching the football game, and they are paying for these services. Those guys are really making money on this interactive component of the satellite experience and not just talking about it. We can learn from that and apply it in the United States.

Broadband is an area where we think the U.S. will lead, as it has led in the expansion of Internet service and is now leading in the growing penetration of residential broadband connections. In these cases, we believe some of the innovations developed here will eventually get reapplied internationally. So while there are differences internationally, we believe that the world is growing smaller and that innovations in one region are usually quickly adapted to other parts of the globe.

Government Regulation

The government plays a very significant role in regulation of the licensing and regulation of the spectrum. We believe that the best approach for government is to move quickly to ensure that consumers are not denied valuable services and companies are able to realize returns on their investments. Of course, any regulatory process needs to be thoughtful and prudent, but protracted waiting periods for decisions on licenses don't really serve either consumers or the business community.

Wireless Winners

Successful companies in all industries thrive because they provide a benefit or fulfill a need that their customers are willing to pay for. In the satellite space, Direct TV and Echostar are successful because they have a service that is affordable and high value added. They deliver a spectacular selection of all digital programming with superior customer service. They came up with very good ideas, they got through the licensing hurdles, they secured the spectrum, and they built the technology. Today they have 15 million satellite customers. In about a one year period, they've added the equivalent to a medium-sized cable company's entire subscriber base. Between them, they add about a quarter of a million customers a month.

In the satellite broadband space, consumers want affordable pricing, a high speed connection to the Internet and they want it available where they live. They want it all, and the companies with the infrastructure to deliver it all will thrive.

Co-existence of Broadband Applications

No question that they'll co-exist and each one will have its own niche. Consumers care about the benefits that matter to them individually. They don't care about the technology that delivers it. Some people will opt for cable, others for DSL and some for satellite. Speed of service, pricing, availability of certain broadband applications, customer service, bundling with other telecom or TV services, and access to service will factor into the individual consumer's choice. In fact, the competition to earn the consumer's business will be the driver for each segment to improve their value proposition.

Keys to Success

I believe the 3 most important things are 1) establishing a low-cost platform that enables affordable pricing; 2) staying focused on the right markets and the right opportunities 3) making it easy for the consumer, from ease-of-installation to reliable service to a world-class customer service organization. First, the consumer will not pay for a company's bloated cost structure. Competition ensures that. That's why enabling affordable pricing to the consumer drives everything from our next generation spot beam architecture to the use of standard components in our low cost modems. Second, we need to invest our resources where we can fill an unmet need. Our offering will be more appealing in areas where consumers don't have access to DSL or cable modem service, so that's where we will focus marketing resources. Third, we must never forget we are in a service business and that our customers have a choice. Most subscribers of satellite TV can receive cable service. One reason they choose satellite is superior customer service. So, cost consciousness, focus on areas with the most opportunities and customer–centric will be the watchwords of our industry.

Moore is one of the relatively few presidents and CEOs who might alternately function as their company's chief technical officer. Instrumental in the creation of the Data Over Cable System Interface Specification (DOCSIS), Moore has patents pending in that technology. This cable-modem specification is now a worldwide standard and the basis for modern cable-modem design by manufacturers such as Bay Networks, Cisco, Toshiba, Thompson, 3Com, Broadcom and Conexant.

Prior to taking his position with WildBlue in October 1998, Moore was vice president of integrated service architecture at Cable Television Laboratories (CableLabs). In this position, he directed technical development in the areas of quality of service (QoS), enhanced services architecture design, traffic engineering, and support for enhanced services such as streaming media (audio/video), IP telephony, and interactive gaming across cable networks. This effort included design of the DOCSIS cable-modem technology, PacketCable(r) QoS architectures and specification, protocol performance simulation and economic analysis of integrated services on shared media cable networks.

Moore holds a master's degree in business administration with distinction from Harvard Business School. He also holds a master's degree in telecommunications engineering (with honors) from the University of Colorado, where his research focused on broadband media access control protocols, Asynchronous Transfer Mode (ATM) and MPEG I and II.

About Inside the Minds

Become a Part of
Inside the Minds

Ask a Question in an Upcoming Book, Nominate an Executive, Post Comments on the Topics Mentioned, Read Expanded Excerpts, Free Excerpts From Upcoming Books

www.InsideTheMinds.com

Inside the Minds was conceived in order to give readers actual insights into the leading minds of business executives worldwide. Because so few books or other publications are actually written by executives in industry, *Inside the Minds* presents an unprecedented look at various industries and professions never before available. In addition, the *Inside the Minds* web site makes the reading experience interactive by enabling readers to post messages and interact with each other, ask questions in upcoming books, read expanded comments on the topics covered and nominate individuals for upcoming books. *Inside the Minds* is now expanding the series to share the wealth of knowledge locked inside the minds of leading executives in every industry worldwide.

Also from Aspatore Books:
Bigwig Briefs
Condensed Business Intelligence From Industry Insiders

Become a Part of *Bigwig Briefs*

Publish a Knowledge Excerpt on an Upcoming Topic (50-5,000 words), Submit an Idea to Write an Entire Bigwig Brief, Post Comments on the Topics Mentioned, Read Expanded Excerpts, Free Excerpts From Upcoming Briefs

www.BigwigBriefs.com

Bigwig Briefs features condensed business intelligence from industry insiders and are the best way for business professionals to stay on top of the most pressing issues. There are two types of *Bigwig Briefs* books: the first is a compilation of excerpts from various executives on a topic, while the other is a book written solely by one individual on a specific topic. *Bigwig Briefs* is also the first interactive book series for business professionals whereby individuals can submit excerpts (50 to 5,000 words) for upcoming briefs on a topic they are knowledgeable on (submissions must be accepted by our editorial review committee and if accepted they receive a free copy of the book) or submit an idea to write an entire Bigwig Brief (accepted ideas/manuscripts receive a standard royalty deal). *Bigwig Briefs* is revolutionizing the business book market by providing the highest quality content in the most condensed format possible for business book readers worldwide.

ASPATORE
BUSINESS REVIEW

The Quarterly Book Featuring Excerpts From the Best Business Books

Aspatore Business Review is the perfect way for busy professionals to stay on top of the most pressing business issues. Each *Aspatore Business Review* includes knowledge excerpts and highlights from best selling business books, in-depth interviews with leading executives, and special features on emerging issues in the workplace. Every quarter, *Aspatore Business Review* brings you the most important excerpts from the best business books on topics such as:

- Management and Leadership
- Technology and the Internet
- Team Building
- Financial Accountability
- Staying ahead of Changing Markets
- Fostering Innovation
- Brand Building

Aspatore Business Review is the one book every business professional should read, and is the best way to keep current with your business reading in the most time efficient manner possible.

Subscribe today to Aspatore Business Review

www.Aspatore.com

ORDER THESE OTHER GREAT BOOKS TODAY!
Great for Yourself or Your Entire Team
Visit Your Local Bookseller Today!

Inside the Minds: Internet Bigwigs
Industry Experts Forecast the Future of the Internet Economy - *Inside the Minds: Internet Bigwigs* includes interviews with a handful of the leading minds of the Internet and technology revolution. These individuals include executives from Excite (Founder), Beenz.com (CEO), Organic (CEO), Agency.com (Founder), Egghead (CEO), Credite Suisse First Boston (Internet Analyst), CIBC (Internet Analyst) and Sandbox.com. Items discussed include killer-apps for the 21st century, the stock market, emerging industries, international opportunities, and a plethora of other issues affecting anyone with a "vested interest" in the Internet and technology revolution. $27.95

Inside the Minds: Leading Women
What it Takes for Women to Succeed and Have it All in the 21st Century - *Inside the Minds: Leading Women* includes interviews with CEOs and executives from companies such as Prudential, Women's Financial Network, SiliconSalley.com, Barclays Global Investors, RealEco.com, AgentArts, Kovair, MsMoney.com, LevelEdge and AudioBasket. These highly acclaimed women explain how to balance personal and professional lives, set goals, network, start a new company, learn the right skills for career advancement and more. $27.95

Inside the Minds: Internet Marketing
Industry Experts Reveal the Secrets to Marketing, Advertising, and Building a Successful Brand on the Internet - *Inside the Minds: Internet Marketing* includes interviews with leading marketing VPs from some of the top Internet companies in the world including Buy.com, 24/7 Media, DoubleClick, Guerrilla Marketing, Viant, MicroStrategy, MyPoints.com, WineShopper.com, Advertising.com and eWanted.com. Their experiences, advice, and stories provide an unprecedented look at the various online and offline strategies involved with building a successful brand on the Internet for companies in every industry. Also examined is calculating return on investment, taking an offline brand online, taking an online brand offline, where the future of Internet marketing is heading, and numerous other issues. $27.95

Inside the Minds: Venture Capitalists
Inside the High Stakes and Fast Paced World of Venture Capital - *Inside the Minds: Venture Capitalists* includes interviews with leading partners from Softbank, ICG, Sequoia Capital, CMGI, New Enterprise Associates, Bertelsmann Ventures, TA Associates, Kestrel Venture Management, Blue Rock Capital, Novak Biddle Venture Partners, Mid-Atlantic Venture Funds, Safeguard Scientific, Divine interVentures, and Boston Capital Ventures. Learn how some of the best minds behind the Internet revolution value companies, assess business models, and identify opportunities in the marketplace. $27.95

Inside the Minds: The Wireless Industry
Industry Leaders Discuss the Future of the Wireless Revolution - *Inside the Minds: The Wireless Industry* includes interviews with leading CEOs from companies such as AT & T Wireless, Omnisky, Wildblue, AirPrime, Digital Wireless, Aperto Networks, Air2Web, LGC Wireless, Arraycomm, Informio and Extenta. Items discussed include the future of the wireless industry, wireless devices, killer-apps in the wireless industry, the international landscape, government issues and more. $27.95

Inside the Minds: The New Health Care Industry
Industry Leaders Discuss the Internet Health Care Revolution - *Inside the Minds: The New Health Care Industry* includes interviews with leading CEOs from companies such as iMcKesson, Medscape, Adam.com, PhaseForward, AthenaHealth.com, HealthGrades, Oncology.com, Scheduling.com, eHealthInsurance and HealthGate Data. Items discussed include the effect of technology on the health care industry, future killer-apps, privacy issues, and the future of health care for patients. $27.95

Inside the Minds: Internet CFOs
Information Every Entrepreneur, Employee, Investor, and Services Professional Should Know About the Financial Side of Internet Companies – *Inside the Minds: Internet CFOs* includes interviews with leading CFOs from Hoovers, CBS Marketwatch, Register.com, eMusic.com webMethods, Ashford.com, Agillion.com, LivePerson, Nerve.com and Edgar Online. Items discussed include the way Internet companies are valued today and in the future, stock options, and financial trends affecting Internet companies at every level. $27.95

Inside the Minds: Internet BizDev
Industry Experts Reveal the Secrets to Inking Deals in the Internet Industry - *Inside the Minds: Internet BizDev* includes interviews with leading business development executives from companies such as Imandi, Real Names, yesmail.com, Netcreations, LifeMinders, Digital Owl, WebCT and Keen.com. Items discussed include calculating potential return on investment, partnership strategies, joint ventures, and where the future of Internet business development is heading among numerous other issues. $27.95

Inside the Minds: Chief Technology Officers
Industry Experts Reveal the Secrets to Developing, Implementing, and Capitalizing on the Best Technologies in the World - *Inside the Minds: Chief Technology Officers* includes interviews with leading technology executives from companies such as Engage, Datek, Symantec, Verisign, Vignette, WebMD, SONICblue, Kana Communications, Flooz.com and The Motley Fool. Their experiences, advice, and research provide an unprecedented look at the various strategies involved with developing, implementing, and capitalizing on the best technologies in the world for companies of every size and in every industry. $27.95

Inside the Minds: Internet Lawyers
The Most Up to Date Handbook of Important Answers to Issues Facing Every Entrepreneur, Lawyer, and Anyone with a Web Site – *Inside the Minds: Internet Lawyers* includes interviews with leading lawyers from some of the top Internet and technology focused law firms in the world. Items discussed include structuring ownership, raising money, venture capital, patents, intellectual property, forming the board, product liability, human resources, stock options, partnership contracts, privacy, and other issues that every business (and their lawyers) should be aware of. $27.95

Bigwig Briefs: Management & Leadership
Industry Experts Reveal the Secrets How to Get There, Stay There, and Empower Others That Work For You
Bigwig Briefs: Management & Leadership includes excerpts of advice from some of the leading executives in the business world. These highly acclaimed executives explain how to break into higher ranks of management, how to become invaluable to your company, and how to empower your team to perform to their utmost potential. (102 Pages) $14.95

Bigwig Briefs: Human Resources & Building a Winning Team
Industry Experts Reveal the Secrets to Hiring, Retaining Employees, Fostering Teamwork, and Building Winning Teams of All Sizes
Bigwig Briefs: Human Resources & Building a Winning Team includes excerpts of advice from some of the leading executives in the business world. These highly acclaimed executives explain the secrets behind hiring the best employees, incentivizing and retaining key employees, building teamwork, maintaining stability, encouraging innovation, and succeeding as a group. (102 Pages) $14.95

Bigwig Briefs: Online Advertising
Industry Experts Reveal the Secrets to Successful Online Advertising Programs
Bigwig Briefs: Online Advertising includes excerpts of advice from some of the leading marketing and advertising executives in the world. These highly acclaimed executives explain the secrets behind strategic planning, implementing, and maximizing your online advertising dollars. (102 Pages) $14.95

Bigwig Briefs: Startups Keys to Success
Industry Experts Reveal the Secrets to Launching a Successful New Venture
Bigwig Briefs: Startups Keys to Success includes excerpts of advice from some of the leading VCs, CEOs CFOs, CTOs and business executives in every industry. These highly acclaimed executives explain the secrets behind the financial, marketing, business development, legal, and technical aspects of starting a new venture. (102 Pages) $14.95

Bigwig Briefs: Small Business Internet Advisor
Industry Experts Reveal the Secrets to Internet Marketing, BizDev, HR, Financing, eCommerce and Other Important Topics Facing Every Small Business Doing Business on the Internet
Bigwig Briefs: Small Business Internet Advisor includes excerpts of advice from some of the leading executives in the world in every field of specialty. These highly acclaimed executives explain the secrets behind making the most of your small business online in a very easy to understand and straight forward fashion. (102 Pages) $14.95

Bigwig Briefs: The Golden Rules of the Internet Economy
Industry Experts Reveal the Best Advice Ever on Succeeding in the Internet Economy
Bigwig Briefs: The Golden Rules of the Internet Economy includes excerpts of advice from some of the leading business executives in the Internet and Technology industries. These highly acclaimed executives explain where the future of the Internet economy is heading, mistakes to avoid for companies of all sizes, and the keys to long term success. (102 Pages) $14.95

Go to www.InsidetheMinds.com for a Complete List of Titles!

About Aspatore Books
www.Aspatore.com

Aspatore Books has become one of the leading book publishing houses in record setting time by combining the best aspects of traditional book publishing with the new abilities enabled by the Internet and technology. Aspatore Books publishes the Inside the Minds, Bigwig Briefs, OneHourWiz and Aspatore Business Review imprints in addition to other best selling non-fiction and fiction books. Aspatore Books is focused on infusing creativity, innovation and interaction into the book publishing industry and providing a heightened experience for readers worldwide. Aspatore Books focuses on publishing traditional print books, while our two portfolio companies, Big Brand Books and Publishville.com focus on developing areas within the book publishing world. Aspatore Books is committed to providing our readers, authors, bookstores, distributors and customers with the highest quality books, book related services, and publishing execution available anywhere in the world.

About Big Brand Books

Big Brand Books assists leading companies and select individuals with book writing, publisher negotiations, book publishing, book sponsorship, worldwide book promotion and generating a new revenue stream from publishing. The goal of Big Brand Books is to help our clients capture the attention of prospective customers, retain loyal clients and penetrate new target markets by sharing valuable information in books and providing the highest quality content for readers worldwide. For more information please visit www.BigBrandBooks.com or email jonp@bigbrandbooks.com.

About Publishville.com

At Publishville.com, individuals worldwide can electronically publish books, articles, speeches, plays, reports, and more, set their own price, earn 50% royalties, and make a name for themselves. Publishville.com also features "The World's Most Intriguing Bookstore" which contains thousands of works from writers worldwide on every topic imaginable available only at Publishville.com.